The Beginning of God's Story

A Commentary on the Book of Genesis

By W.J. Sturm

Scripture quotations are generally taken from the King James Bible.

Some Scripture quotations are taken from the New King James Version®, Copyright © 1982 by Thomas Nelson, Inc. (and those few out-of-sequence footnotes in those passages are particular footnotes retained from the NKJV.)

To my friends in the Chapel Class at Berean Baptist Church,
who endured some 90 weeks of my teaching on Genesis...

Thank you for finding reasons to stay.

Preface

A greater portion of this material was taught in the setting expressed in the dedication. The remained was preached in perhaps 5 additional settings in my current ministry. I recommend that you get a hold of my Matthew Commentary for more background on that setting.

Introduction

Acts 7 reminds us that Moses was an informed Egyptian, raised in royalty. All the tools needed to effectively write this record were his. Then, as Exodus 3 tells us, Moses spends his 2nd set of 40 years with another leader—Jethro, sometimes called a priest.

Luke 16:26-31 tells us that Abraham believed there were two divisions in the Old Testament: "Moses and the prophets." Other than Luke 24 where we have a third division called the Psalms, but in any case, Moses is mentioned first.

As it applies to authorship, it seems like John 1 makes the best case because, at the end of the chapter, Philip tells Nathaniel that Moses wrote about Jesus. When Jesus sees Him he makes a very clear reference to Himself from Genesis 28. If that was Jesus confirming what Philip said for Nathaniel's sake, then Jesus is telling us that Moses wrote Genesis 28…and by extension, all of Genesis.

Even though somebody may disagree with us on authorship, they probably know why. Here's a sampling:

1. Genesis 12:6 tells us that at least part of Genesis was written when the "Canaanite was [not] in the land." Well, Moses was dead by that time. So it looks like somebody added to Genesis.
2. Genesis 14:14 tells us that there was a place called "Dan." It is probable that since Moses never saw this come to fruition from the tribes themselves in Canaan, that Moses did not write this. Again, he was dead by this time.
3. Genesis 36:31 implies that the writer is in a time when there "was" a king in Israel. This happened after Moses died.

4. Deuteronomy 34 tells us that Moses died and it discusses his burial. It is most natural to say that somebody else wrote this.

Yet, if somebody "generally writes" the body of literature, they get the credit for authorship.

Chapter 1

1:1[1]

In the [a]beginning [b]God created the heavens and the earth.[2]
Proverbs 16:4 speaks of "all things" being "created for Himself" while Revelation 4:11 says "all things"—along with ourselves— are here for God's pleasure…God's pleasure. This, then, is the beginning to God's story.

Remember that the **heavens** are created on day 2 while **earth** is created on day 3. This, then, is a summary verse—along with 2:1. All things and all things within those things are made in these next six days of creation (2:1; Exodus 20:11). Yes, angels too. They count. The earth and heavens…yes, they too.

1:2-5

3 Then God said, "Let there be light"[3] Some have said that this is Jesus (since there are no sources for light until day 4), but this seems unnecessary.

4 And God saw the light, Perhaps it should be pointed out that this is a creation of that which scientists say is "light-years-old light" between the earth and the light's source. In other words, the light was created on day one and it is, then, merely appearing as "aged" to the observer today. Adam is another great argument that God creates things with a mere appearance of age. Adam looked like an adult when he was a mere second old.

---

[1]See also under 1:20-23.
[a]Ps. 102:25; John 1:1–3; Heb. 1:10
[b]Gen. 2:4; Ps. 8:3; Acts 17:24; Rom. 1:20; Heb. 1:2; 11:3; Rev. 4:11
[2]Some might be surprised to know that it was in the late 70's that the Pope of the Catholic church mused that what we are here reading (really the first 11 chapters of Genesis) are simply myth. Listen here: http://www.aloha.net/~mikesch/darwin.htm [accessed July 31, 2017].
[3]See more from my commentary on 2 Corinthians (4:6).

Having said all of this, Paul did say that this was a picture of Jesus.[4] Colossians 1:15-18 even go as far as to say "all things were created by [Jesus] and for [Jesus]." Think about that. He made these here, and He made them for Himself. We are not surprised by any of this since Jesus told us that "Moses" was about Him (Luke 24:44). Of course, if this is true, then the Bible is not a science textbook, but a book concerning redemption.

5 God called the light Day, and the darkness He called Night. So the evening and the morning were the first day. While I cannot prove that the days were 24 hours long, I can tell you that it was one rotation of the earth long: **evening and morning.**

1:6-10[5]

Then God said, "Let there be a firmament in the midst of the waters, Job 26:8 and following seem to say that there is a sea and cloud around the throne of God (and Revelation 4 says so too).[6] It is possible, then, that "water above the **firmament**" is at the edge of the universe. It could be that this is not much water if the universe is cone-shaped. Psalm 148 does speak of this very same water "above the heavens." This water was still there at the time of this writing so it doesn't seem feasible that this is simply "antedeluvian" storehouse. **and let it divide the waters from the waters."** This is our second act of separation (the first being "light from darkness"). This will show up again as the ceiling below the rain (Genesis 7:11-12; Job 26:8-11; Psalm 148:1-6).

8 And God called the firmament Heaven. So the evening and

---

[4]See my commentary on 2 Corinthians 4.

[5]See under 1:20-23 as well.

[6]It makes me a little nervous to clarify poetry (like Job) with symbolism (like Revelation).

A rainbow is also around the throne [see this commentary (chapter 9) and my commentary on Revelation (chapter 4)].

the morning were the second day. Some have said this was a temporary barrier and source of ante-deluvian water—a sort of canopy around the earth that "then was" (2 Peter 3:6). So a sort of convex object arises out of the water with water trapped above?

There are other explanations. "Heavens" of verse 1 don't even show up in the chronology of the six days' creation until now. So this is the "creation of 'heavens'". It seems, from a spherical earth perspective, this would be an ever expanding "outer space" which are even big enough to contain the products of "day 4" and low enough to contain the birds (day 5).

Then, others could say that the Scripture contains a flat-earth perspective and that the firmament is an obvious, existing canopy that now is.

1:11

Then God said, "Let the earth bring forth grass, the herb that yields seed, and the fruit tree that yields fruit according to its kind, whose seed is in itself, on the earth"; so plants that have seeds and plants that have fruit that have seeds. **and it was so.**

1:14[7]

Then God said, "Let there be lights in the firmament of the heavens is it from the perspective of the author and that the lights are **in the firmament** only from the perspective of the writer? If not, then the **firmament** is expansive enough to have all the heavenly bodies and yet…water is contained above it (day 2),[8] and the birds are also in the **firmament** according to day 5. Psalm 19:1-4 says the **firmament** is the "heavens" and actually contains

---

[7]See also under 1:20-23 for 1:14-17.

[8]It could be that the water is above the firmament like one's head could be "under water" without being in the concrete "under" the swimming pool. In other words, the water is anywhere above the lowest limit of the firmament.

the sun. Daniel 12:3 also says that the stars are in **the firmament.**

to divide the day from the night; It seems, then, that light of day 1 is what has been already performing this function.

1:16

Then God made two great lights: the greater light the sun loses 4,600,000 tons of mass per second, I am told. Pretty massive and yet 74,000,000 of them would fit in the star Anteras in the Skorpio constellation **to rule the day, and the lesser light to rule the night.** Perhaps Moses' desire to not use the names of Egyptian deities prompted these strange terms of **greater light and lesser light.**

He made the stars also. This is absurd. It's like saying, "

a) "He dug the Panama canal (impressive); he dug the basin of Lake Hickory (wow); he built the Hoover dam (incredible)....and He (shrugging) carved out the Grand Canyon."

b) "He painted the ceiling of the Sistine chapel (beautiful); he painted the Mona Lisa (exquisite); he crafted the peacock in the zoo (marvelous)....and He (click the tongue) chiseled Mount Rushmore."

So, we say that the earth was here before the stars without any hesitation.

1. <u>God's focus is on the planet.</u>
In the Babylonian cosmogony Enuma Elish the stars have a prominent role, but in the Genesis account the creation of the stars is treated almost as an aside, downplaying their role in God's sight. The Hebrew text simply adds afterward, as if a mere afterthought—"and the stars" (1:16).[9]

2. <u>God's focus is on the planet's people.</u> The universe is for all those who would become the crown of God's creation on day 6. So there's no need to search for extraterrestrial life, and we need to stop feeling small. After all, He spends more time on day 6 than He does on all previous five days combined, much less "day 4." "The stars are the big deal, and we play into its plan," says the astrologist,[10] but God says, "I count mankind a much bigger deal." The stars point to us and observe us; not us, the stars. They observe such sublime reality that the real image bearers of God are not blobs of gas but those of Genesis 1:26-28 that we are in His image:

3.   <u>God's focus is on the Son</u> more than on our troubles. The righteous Adam Who made right the wrongs of the awful fall of our fathers (Romans 5; 1 Corinthians 15). The One Who is the full-on, unfallen, untainted image of God (Colossians 1:15). It is here when the preacher realizes that it isn't even our big ideas or plans or dreams or even…our heartaches that are the masterpiece or the prize. No, it is news of a sin crusher (Genesis 3:15).

> ***He made the stars also***, *which are here spoken of as they appear to vulgar eyes, without distinguishing between the planets and the fixed stars, or accounting for their number, nature, place, magnitude, motions, or influences; for the scriptures were written, not to gratify our curiosity and make us astronomers, but to lead us to God [through Christ], and make us saints.[11]*

---

[9] K. A. Mathews, *Genesis 1-11:26*, vol. 1A, The New American Commentary (Nashville: Broadman & Holman Publishers, 1996), 154–155.
[10] More here: http://www.sermonaudio.com/search.asp?subsetitem=Astrology&subsetcat=series&keyword=bereanbaptistch&SourceOnly=true&includekeywords=&ExactVerse= [accessed June 5, 2017].
[11] Matthew Henry, *Matthew Henry's Commentary on the Whole Bible:*

1:17-18

18 and to rule not the same as "dominion" in verse 26, however it is the same as the one in 3:16. This is not dominating; this is governing.

1:20-23[12]

Then God said, "Let the waters abound with an abundance of living ⁵creatures, and let birds fly above the earth across the face of the firmament The same word used as the objective of the 2nd day of Creation (1:6-8), and it is called **heavens**. **Firmament** is also the word used on the 4th day (1:14-17) as the arena which was filled with the lights created on that day. **of the heavens."** This is the word used in the summaries of 1:1 and 2:1. It is also considered one and the same with **firmament** (1:8) and was therefore created on day 2. Once again, we have an argument against the gap theory: What is used as a summary of creation week in 1:1 and 2:1 is deemed as a summary of the whole of creation because it is actually a component of creation during the week…namely, "Day 2."

Then, if there were actually a "splitting of hairs" over what **across the face of the firmament** actually meant (whether the birds flew in the **firmament** or actually just appeared to do so as they perhaps flew below the **firmament** but merely **across the face of the firmament),** 1:26, 1:28, and 1:30 actually call the birds the "birds of the heavens"[13] (translated "air" in many versions). This is just

---

Complete and Unabridged in One Volume (Peabody: Hendrickson, 1994), 5.
[12]See my commentary on Luke (footnote under 9:18-36).
⁵souls
[13] "H8064 - shamayim - Strong's Hebrew Lexicon (KJV)." Blue Letter Bible. Web. 2 Aug, 2017.
<https://www.blueletterbible.org//lang/lexicon/lexicon.cfm?Strongs=H8064&t=KJV>.

like saying the "birds of the firmament."

So, the **firmament of the heavens** then is not only high enough to contain the lights, but is low enough to contain the birds.

Now then, day 5 provides that which fills what was created in day 2 much like that which was created on day 4 filled what was created on day 1. The source of light filled the light that would emanate from it: mysterious, I know. Of course, man and land animals were created on day 6 to fill what was created on day 3.

21 So ^wGod created great sea creatures and every living thing that moves, with which the waters Interesting that, unlike the "heavens (day 2) and earth (day 3)", we're not told anything about the creation of the water (much less the basin upon which it rests which we would call a "planet").

22 And God blessed them, saying, I hesitate to write this because of what it may imply, but **God blessed** the fish and the birds before man was even around. I am also reminded that God spoke to serpents (Genesis 3), donkeys (Numbers 22-24), and whales (Jonah 2). **"Be fruitful and multiply, and fill the waters in the seas, and let birds multiply on the earth."** So much for a concern of over-population. He said "fill them!"

1:26-29[14]

"Let Us make man This is the word *adam* in the Hebrew and is one of the four uses for that Hebrew word in the Old Testament. So, it is the common word for "mankind."[15] **in Our image,** Herein

---

^wPs. 104:25–28

[14]See also under 1:16, 1:17-18, 1:20-23, 2:1-3, & 2:8-9.

[15]"adam" is the name of a city on the Jordan River (Josh 3:16). It is also a word that speaks primarily of the male gender (Genesis 2:18-21). It fourthly speaks, with the Hebrew def article, it speaks of a particular "man" (Genesis 2:24).

lies the biggest problem with abortion. Who decides at what point the zygote or embryo or fetus is an **image** bearer?

Anyway, we are in his **image**…

1. Expressively ("God said")
2. Volitionally ("Let")
3. Relationally ("Let us")
4. Creatively ("make")[16]
5. Administratively ("let them have dominion")
6. Reproductively ("be fruitful")
7. Emotionally ("it was good")
8. Individually ("none suitable")

according to Our likeness; In this time, around the life of the writer Moses, Sovereigns and rulers of land would put **likenesses** of themselves all over His kingdom so that one might know when they are taking their lives and destinies into their own hands by trespassing into another king's realm. It may also be a welcomed site for a weary traveler to come closer to a king's realm and see these big stones or bronze images on the borders of a great nation. They may have traveled miles and miles to get to the king, and look, on the borders and corners of his realm would be **images** and **likenesses** of that very powerful and fearful king. When you arrived you had to realize right away that He had dominion over all things in his kingdom.

When our Creator created, not stone statues like later kings were found to do, but breathing, animated men and women, they were His image bearers, and they were to **them have dominion[17] over**

---

[16]Here's a boy who decided to be creative: http://www.sermonaudio.com/sermoninfo.asp?SID=62131745291 [accessed August 10, 2017].

[17]This trail also ends in Revelation 5:9-10, covered in my commentary on Revelation where there is subjugation of all people groups both around the throne and in front of the throne (Revelation 7:12 and following in the same

the fish of the sea, over the birds of the air, and over the cattle, over all the earth and over every creeping thing that creeps on the earth." Why? "the earth is the Lord's and its fullness" (Psalm 24:1).

It is here summarized for us again. The conversation took place among God (mysterious enough) and the summary from the writer here begins: **27 So God created man in His own image; in the image of God He created him; male and female He created them.** This tells us that most of the 2nd chapter of Genesis takes place in this sixth day...unless you believe there was a **female** before Eve (who is found in chapter 2). It's hard to imagine, but there are many, many views about how we should see this historical Adam and Eve (as found in these first three chapters).[18]

Then God blessed them, and God said to them, "Be fruitful and multiply; fill the earth All of the "lesser beings" who are not in God's image are subject to those who are God's image. So, two results of God's creative act: 1. All the other creatures fear God because they fear His image, and 2. All the image bearers are to be sub-regents of the earth—controlling and subjugating the earth as the One Who cast His image upon them. **and subdue it;** ultimately and spiritually fulfilled in Gospel domination [see my commentary on Mark (16:15)].

28 have dominion over the fish of the sea, over the birds of the air, and over every living thing that moves on the earth." All Creatures: **fish of the sea, birds of the air (firmament), every living thing that moves on the earth.**

We find out in **1:29-31** that 1. God was pleased with the way He designed everything;[19] 2. The animals were to be subject to the

---

commentary).
    [18]The ramifications of which are discussed here:
http://www.sermonaudio.com/sermoninfo.asp?SID=1120141221257 [accessed 8/1/17].

image bearers but not fearing them in the way they do today (eating the similar things); 3. Something, therefore, has gone horribly wrong, and the image of the Sovereign was marred. Now all the things we listed before are damaged and we now only dream of a perfected state…and it won't be long.

But maybe we should list the legacy of this Adam, and see their perfections in Christ:

1. Both slept deeply on the eve of the Sabbath (Mark 15:42).
2. The death he died[20] by sinning (Genesis 2:17) as revealed in the isolation he felt from God (3:9-10). Jesus, on the other hand experienced the woes of isolation from His Father (Mark 15:34).

We go forward to Genesis 3:15 and we see that while man is now cursed with his family and with his ground, there is a grand promise of a great comeback and a crushing of a serpent's head. I wonder who? I wonder…when? Who could possibly reign the whole world and become the ruler and dominator of creation now that Adam and his family have no hope?

Isaiah 52:7-10 gives us the answer. When will the earth "see the salvation of God?" When the "watchmen lift up their voices" and "bring glad tidings" "proclaiming 'Your God reigns'?"

The language of Mark 1:3 and the message of Mark 1:14-15 speaks the same.

The message of John is preparation for a king and the king

---

[19]It should be noted, then, that God—the Supreme Designer and Enjoyer of His Work—is the Greatest Sufferer. Listen for more: http://www.sermonaudio.com/sermoninfo.asp?SID=42115125210 [accessed August 10, 2017].

[20]Genesis 20 teaches us (in "you are a dead man") that Adam was as "good as dead" or "on death row" for at least 800 years (Genesis 5:3-5).

introduces the Gospel, and the reason the kingdom is being compared with all the seeds of the earth (Mark 4:31) is because of the implication that it will in fact, marvelously and miraculously cover the whole earth. Here is reference—another hint—"the birds of the air" (a Genesis 1:26-28 reference).

We get a little hint in Mark 9:1, with the help of Mark 16:15 and Acts 1:8 that this is a promise of Pentecost. When they were empowered to take the Gospel to the entire world. Probably, there is a little help here to clarify Matthew's version (Matthew 16:27-28) with an A.D. culmination of the shift between Jerusalem and Heavenly Zion which lasted 40 years (a generation).[21]

> *Mark 11:8-10 And many spread their clothes on the road, and others cut down leafy branches from the trees and spread them on the road. 9 Then those who went before and those who followed cried out, saying: "Hosanna! 'Blessed is He who comes in the name of the LORD!' 10* **Blessed is the kingdom of our father David** *That comes in the name of the Lord! Hosanna in the highest!"*

Here we see that all the kingdoms of Israel past were shadows of and progenitors to the kingdom of the king who would be born to the lineage of King David. Why were we expecting a King? Because God has always had a king (Psalm 2:1-7), and always planned for a king (Deuteronomy 17:17) to be born to King David and have a reign that would never end (2 Samuel 7:16; Isaiah 9:6-7), and that His King would reign over the entire world (Psalm 24). We have been expecting it since Genesis 49's promise of a "scepter from Judah." We have been expecting it since Numbers 24's promise that a "star would arise from Jacob," and it continued right on through to palm Sunday here when Israel's greatest hope was God's king reigning on God's earth. It has always been good news that a perfect kingdom would come to this earth and it has

---

[21]See more in my commentary on Matthew.

17

always been the prayer of God's people (most obviously taught through the Lord's Prayer of Matthew 6).

Well, I wonder what will serve as the image bearers of this King and His new Kingdom? I wonder Who will take these images around the globe so that all creatures will be subject to Him? I wonder how these creatures will be subjected through these who will take His image, establishing His reign over the earth?

We have our term Gospel of the Kingdom (Mark 1:14-15; 13:9-10; 14:8-9), and look…it must be everywhere. Why? Because that has always been the plan: world domination by the righteous king promised in Genesis 3:15; 12:3 ("all nations").

With the news from Jesus that He must give His life as a ransom (Mark 10:45) and this talk of a burial, we get the idea now that the King, Who's ever-increasing reign over the whole of creation following the news of this reign must first die…and that it is, says Mark 1:1, part of this Gospel: "The Creator's Son dies for His Creation."

1:30[22]

---

[22]See also under 1:20-23.

Chapter 2

heaven and earth Provide us the summary statement for the introductory statement of 1:1.

2 and on the seventh day God ended His work which He had made; and He rested on the seventh day from all His work which He had made. Exodus 20:10-11 show us that this was the Sabbath day., which means "intermission."[24] God, then, took a Sabbath. **3 Then God blessed the seventh day and sanctified it, because in it He rested from all His work which God had created and made.** Said a 3ʳᵈ time in these last two verses. We should see that this word is used in other words…like music. You can "rest" for a musical measure and not be tired. It's just time for you to not exert energy in the manner of producing a note. In other words, since God wasn't tired, He must be teaching something through His example.

Then God blessed the seventh I would argue that the Bible uses the number seven more often for completeness than proposed "perfection." "Completeness" because it's when things are done. All the way back on the seven days of creation, the seventh day he rested because he was done. The **seven**th day is the Sabbath. The **seven**th time that they marched around Jericho was when the walls fell. **Seven** times Namaan dipped in the Jordan River to be healed of leprosy; **seven** years of plenty in Egypt; **seven** years of famine followed that (in Joseph's time); **seven** years of Nebuchadnezzar when he went insane in the wilderness; seven petitions in the Lord's prayer; **seven** parables in Matthew 13 that are told by Jesus; **seven**

---

[23]See also under 1:20-23; See also my commentary on Zephaniah 3:14-17.

[24]"H7676 - shabbath - Strong's Hebrew Lexicon (KJV)." Blue Letter Bible. Web. 9 Apr, 2019. <https://www.blueletterbible.org//lang/lexicon/lexicon.cfm?Strongs=H7676&t=KJV>.

loaves of bread that fed the multitudes as one of Jesus' miracles; **seven** sayings of Jesus on the cross; **seven** deacons of Acts 6; the **seven**s in this book of Revelation.

day and sanctified it set it aside **because in it He rested** though He was not tired.

created and made. Verse 7 contains the word "formed." Is Moses trying to say there were three ways God brought things onto the planet or are these synonyms? 1:26 contains "make" while 1:27 says "created" while 2:7 says "form"—all of them speaking of the very same thing ("man"). These are synonymous.

1. Sabbath is pre-law. Just as those things listed below:
    a. Sabbaths (2:1) before Moses (Exodus 20:11; 34:21).
    b. animal sacrifices (Genesis 4:3-4) before Moses (Leviticus 1-7), and
    c. "clean and unclean" animals (Genesis 7:2) before Moses (Leviticus 11),
    d. death penalty for murders (Genesis 9:6) before Moses (Numbers 35:23),
    e. we have here a **priest**hood before Moses (Leviticus 8),
    f. a "tithe" (Genesis 14:20) before Moses (Leviticus 27:30),
    g. dowry (or bride price) for virgin caught in the field (Genesis 34:1-11) before Moses (Deuteronomy 22:28-29).
    h. and levirate marriage (Genesis 38:1-4) before Moses (Deuteronomy 25:5-10).

2. Sabbath is comparable to baptism in NT: Just as Jesus had no sin of which to repent, God had no weariness from labor for which He needed recovery. It is interesting that in both "beginnings" we have this similarity. A corollary, then, is that we were created for rest. Man has not fallen yet; God

does not need to relax. This day, then, is for us.

3. This makes sense after 6 days of labor, which is the Biblical pattern set here.

    a. So if you are blessed to have a Monday-Friday work schedule, then that means you have a day of rest before the Christian day of worship, the First Day of the week. You have been blessed to have a "work day" for Jesus at the beginning of the week because you have sufficiently rested at the end of your work week on the day before.

    b. What is clear is that there needs to be one day of rest for every 6 days of labor.

    c. Let me then be clear, if you work very hard out of necessity Monday-Saturday, then you must somehow keep Sunday as restful as possible while still fulfilling the Christian expectation of Sunday corporate worship with the body of Christ.

4. God blessed the Sabbath. Are you willing to "un-bless it" and "normalize" what God has blessed and set aside?

"What about Romans 14?" Nobody was seemingly required to keep the Sabbath until Moses' time. Approximately 2500 years between God's keeping of it and the command to men to do the same. More than 1/3 of human history passed before man was required to keep it. It's also not repeated as a requirement to the New Testament believer (contrary to the other 9 commandments). Colossians 2:16 also seems to say Christ is the "substance" while the Sabbath is "the shadow."

However, we must remember what God has done here. While in this book of Genesis we have some main characters (Adam/Eve(3:1-3); Cain/Abel(4); Noah/Shem(5-11); Abraham/Sarah(12-25); Isaac/Ishmael (16-38); Jacob/Esau (25-50); Joseph/Judah (37-50)), we need to remind ourselves that the Main Character is really God and

21

He has **blessed** animals with fruitfulness (1:22). He has blessed man with fruitfulness (1:28), and now He is **bless**ing the Sabbath for our fruitfulness.

5. The Sabbath is the 7th Day:
   a. There are no New Testament references to switching the Sabbath to another day. As a matter of fact, while this reference is as clear as possible to show us that we ought to rest on our Sabbath, there are others in the NT which are clear in saying that believers met on the "First Day of the week."
   b. "I thought Christ was our Sabbath" (usually referencing Colossians 2:16[25] and Hebrews 4).
      i. Yes, having a spiritual rest will make having our physical rest much better.
      ii. However, having Christ ("spiritual rest") does not make us physical supermen. We must still listen to our bodies.
6. Sabbath is not going away. Isaiah 66:21-24 shows us that this will be, in some way, celebrated in the future kingdom, the kingdom to come. It will be at least utilized to count the time.
7. If the Sabbath was needed before the fall for human flourishing, how much more after the fall with its cursed effects (Genesis 3:15-17).[26]

2:4-6[27]

This is the history of the heavens and the earth when they were created, in the day that the LORD God made the earth and the heavens, some parallelism, perhaps a chiasm (**heaven and earth**

---

[25]See my comments on the often utilized Colossians 2:16 in my commentary on Ephesians, Colossians, & Philemon.

[26]I considered this first after hearing it at about 3:00 on this recording: https://podcasts.apple.com/us/podcast/ask-pastor-john/id618132843?i=1000454247214 [accessed 10/26/19].

[27]See also under 2:15-17.

are switched around). **5 before any plant of the field was in the earth and before any herb of the field had grown.** It must not be a blanket statement about vegetation, because there was plenty of that before **rain** or **man.**

6 but a mist went up from the earth and watered the whole face of the ground. Clearly, verses 5 and 6 have something to do with "the history of heavens and earth" so we should be thinking of day 3 primarily and the part which the "heavens" had with "earth" at that time—which we're told in verse 5 here…was very little in regards to rain, but more (now that we know more) to do in regards to day 4: photosynthesis.

2:7[28]

And the LORD God formed man of the dust of the ground, This creation is the 2nd cure for the lack of cultivation activity from verse 5 (the first was that "mist"). Whatever is being described in verse 5, it appears it is a particular type of "plant" and "herb" that was going to be fine without "mist" and without **man.**

and [i]breathed into his nostrils the breath of life; and man meaning "from the ground" **became a living being.** This word is used 42 times in 38 verses and often translated "soul." This should tell us we ought to be very careful getting anthropology here.

2:8-9

The LORD God planted a garden eastward in Eden, and there He put the man could include both "man and woman" (1:26-27). **whom He had formed. 9 And out of the ground the LORD God made every tree grow that is pleasant to the sight and good for food. The tree of life was also in the midst of the garden, and**

---

[28]See under 2:1-3 as well.
[i] Job 33:4

the tree of the knowledge of good and evil. So much for child-proofing everything. In other words, the potential danger existed. Moreover, He made the danger! This means that the potential weakness of man (unlike angels) was built into man by the Creator.

2:10-14

12 And the gold one would wonder if the Egyptian background of the author made this relevant. **of that land is good.**

13 The name of the second river is Gihon; it is the one which goes around the whole land of Cush. Probably Ethiopia. It's important to see that at the time of writing, Moses is using names that then were. In other words, we don't know that the rivers had this name when Adam was placed in the garden. **14 The name of the third river is Hiddekel; it is the one which goes toward the east of [3]Assyria. The fourth river is the Euphrates.** So the Tigris **(Hiddekel)** and the **Euphrates** and it's direction from **Assyria** is given. This presents an issue with either the young earth perspective.[29] In any case, it is helpful to know that these are real locations that existed and can be found today.

2:15-17[30]

Then the LORD God took the man and put him in the garden of Eden to tend and keep a military term as well meaning to protect **it.** Apparently this is the remedy of 2:5-6. Certain things would not be flourishing until man and woman were in garden. He built a dependence for man into some vegetation just like He built in man the need for woman (verse 18).

---

[3] Heb. *Ashshur*

[29]Which supposes that the same Flood that produced the Grand Canyon (not that it occurred over millions of years) did not reroute these miniscule river beds. Somehow, before the flood you could find these same rivers in the same part of the world where they now exist.

[30]See under 1:26-28 also.

17 but of the tree of the knowledge of good and evil you shall not eat, for in the day that you eat of it you shall surely die." Genesis 5:3 shows us Adam was no older than 130 years old when he fell. This hardly leaves time for Cain and Abel to be born, grow up, and for Cain to kill him. Seth is born to replace Abel and Adam lives to be 930 years old and thus lived 800 years or more after he sinned and **died**. This, therefore, does not mean physical death.

Did Adam sin by disregarding God's command to multiply? After all, the first mention of a child is not until Genesis chapter 4? The answer is "no." Looking at Genesis 1:27, the text states that male and female are created in God's image on the same day. Keeping in mind that Moses is writing this in retrospect, one should see 2:15-20, still on Day 6. Adam is in the garden and given yet another command: He must name the animals. In verse 18, God says "I will make" which means Eve was not yet there at that time on day 6. In the timeline of Day 6, God brings the animals to Adam for naming (2:19-20), and then he is put to sleep, still on Day 6. By the end of Day 6, all the animals have been created and named, Adam was made from the ground and Eve was formed from Adam's side. Immediate obedience to "multiply" would not have been possible until Eve was made. Continuing the thoughts that come with the command to multiply, was Eve's curse part of this command? Again the answer is "no." Looking at 3:16, God tells Eve that her sorrow (labor) and conception (pregnancy) will be multiplied, or made great. Therefore, Eve would have previously had the physical quality of labor and pregnancy. Chapter 3 is likely to have come very close in time after chapter 2; since she is not surprised at all by a talking serpent.

2:18-20[31]

And the LORD God said, "It is not good that man should be

---

[31]See also under 2:15-17.

alone; I will make him a helper comparable this proves that woman is not 2nd class compared to the **man.** Jesus was not 2nd class to the Father and we see that 1 Corinthians 11:3 makes these a parallel.

2:24

Therefore a man shall leave his father and mother and be joined to his wife, and they shall become one flesh. This is a narrator's comment, and not the words of Adam. Jesus said God said it (Matthew 19:4-5).

Chapter 3

3:1

Now the serpent identified as Satan (Revelation 12:1-3; 12:9; 20:10) and the devil (John 8:44) **was [b]more cunning than any beast of the field** and yet, he was in the garden. Whether God stood by as the serpent entered the garden or whether God placed it in the garden, God is responsible for what is about to transpire: the moment of temptation.

which the LORD God had made. And he said to the woman, "Has God indeed said, 'You shall not eat of every tree of the garden'?" This is untrue. God told them in chapter two they could actually eat any tree of the garden but one.

3:2-3

And the woman said to the serpent, "We may eat the [c]fruit of the trees of the garden; She doesn't seem surprised (any more than Balaam does that he is talking to a donkey, Numbers 22-24). Of course, she corrects the serpent's error but then adds something, apparently, in the next verse. We may assume that God never forbade their "touching" of it, but that is a minor point. **3 but of the fruit of the tree which *is* in the midst of the garden, God has said, 'You shall not eat it, nor shall you [d]touch it, lest you die.' "** perhaps she thought it was said this way. She didn't hear it from God's mouth, and we are sure that Adam didn't lie to her (or that would have been "the fall").

3:4-5

Then the serpent said to the woman, "You will not surely die.

---

[b]2 Cor. 11:3
[c]Gen. 2:16, 17
[d]Ex. 19:12, 13; Rev. 22:14

27

This dispels the idea that Eve wasn't sure of God's words. She knew He promised death (or else Satan's rebuttal wouldn't make sense). **5 For God knows that in the day you eat of it your eyes will be opened, and you will be like God, knowing good and evil."** This was true. This **God** said so, and is yet an "us" (3:22).

you will be like God just as he himself desired (Isaiah 14:14). He offers to those in God's image that which he himself could not obtain.

3:6-7

So when the woman saw that the tree *was* good here we see something that is sensually **good** (related to the senses) but it is not morally **good.** "This feels/tastes/looks/smells/sounds **good"** is a damnable criteria.

for food, God said it wasn't good for food. **that it *was* pleasant to the eyes, and a tree desirable to make *one* wise, she took of its fruit and ate. She also gave to her husband with her,** he made have actually watched all this take place.

and he ate. It seems as though the three types of sins listed in 1 John 2:16 are here in this verse: "lust of the flesh" led Eve to think she needed it; "lust of the eyes" led Eve to see it as attractive; "pride of life" led Eve to think she knew better than God.

It would be an awful disservice to not even mention the entire purpose of this is to teach us the love of Christ for His bride. See more notes on this in my commentary on Ephesians (5:25-33).

7 Then the eyes of both of them were opened, just as the serpent promised. **and they knew that they *were* naked; and they sewed fig leaves together and made themselves coverings.** Exodus 34:29 talks about a time when Moses couldn't be seen with the eyes of those around him because God's glory radiated from

Moses' skin (Paul also mentions this in 2 Corinthians 3:13). One might wonder if this would have an greater impact if Moses was not clothed (as was the case up until now with Adam and Eve). If so, they were, in fact, clothed…in a sense (just not as we are and not as they were beginning here) with their regular communication with God (as implied in the next verse). So, it seems beginning here the glory of God did not radiate from their skin as God had not been with them while they were involved with the serpent and they "sinned it away" (for lack of a better term) finding themselves **naked.** I will readily say that I don't remember where I read this, but I believe it was John Calvin who said that our clothes today are our fanciest reminders of the fall; or, they are an expensive and lavish display of our failure to obey.

3:8

And they heard the sound of the LORD God walking in the garden in the cool of the day, and Adam and his wife ʲhid themselves when people are guilty and don't wish to be confronted, they hide.

3:9

Then the LORD God called to Adam and said to him, "Where *are* you?" I speak about this in my commentary on Matthew (chapters 22 and 26). God is not seeking information; he is seeking their honesty. This is seen time and time again in the life of Christ, but this happens beforehand in other places like Genesis 4 and 1 Kings 19 and Jonah 4. Even the apostles followed suit in Acts 5.

3:11-14

And He said, "Who told you that you *were* naked? Have you eaten from the tree of which I commanded you that you should

---

ʲJer. 23:24

29

not eat?" Man will one day see this great privilege restored (see my commentary on Revelation and see the table of comparison between Genesis and Revelation). **12 Then the man said, "The woman whom You gave *to be* with me, she gave me of the tree, and I ate."** Adam admits he was not tricked (as Eve does in verse 13). This was a measured choice. It seems as though Adam chose to partake of sin so that he could remain with Eve. This is a sort of picture of Jesus who was counted as a partaker of the sin of His bride so they could stay together forever. Romans 8:4 and Philippians 2:6-8 are phenomenal commentaries on this.

14 So the LORD God said to the serpent: "Because you have done this, You *are* cursed more than all cattle, And more than every beast of the field; On your belly you shall go, Maybe the serpent had legs at this point.

3:15-17[32]

And I will put enmity Between you and the woman, And between your seed and her Seed; Again, Revelation comes into view when you see the "dragon" (Satan, 12:9) persecutes the woman (12:13).

This is also the only time you find the **seed** of the **woman** in the Bible, quite the hint towards the virgin birth.

It also seems that the serpent's seed is as literal as the woman to keep a parallel interpretation. John 17 says that Satan has a son and it is Judas. 1 Timothy 3:16 speaks of Jesus as the mystery of godliness (God manifested in the flesh; He has a son) while 2 Thessalonians 2 speaks of both the "son of perdition" (as John 17) and "the mystery of iniquity" (Satan in the flesh; he has a son?).

See also under 1:16 & 1:26-28.

---

[32]See under 1:17-18 & 2:15-17.

16 To the woman He said: "I will greatly multiply your sorrow and your conception; we see no record that they actually had children before this so it must be that they fell/sinned within close proximity of the 6th day, or else we should assume they simply did not obey 1:26-27 for decades potentially. **In pain you shall bring forth children; Your desire *shall be* for your husband,** in the next chapter we find this same phraseology (4:7) and it has the idea of sin "seeking domination" over Cain. This with the next phrase **And he shall [t]rule over you"** shows us that Eve will engage in a power struggle with her husband [and pass this contentious spirit to all women after her as the "mother of all living" (3:20)].

Rule is not the same word exercised in 1:28. This is not a domination thing; it is a much calmer idea.

17 Then to Adam He said, [u]"Because you have heeded the voice of your wife, and have eaten from the tree [v]of which I commanded you, saying, 'You shall not eat of it': [w]"Cursed *is* the ground for your sake; just as increased pain in labor is the scar for a woman, inefficient work will be the scar for the man. He will work as hard as before and bring forth minimal fruit. Well, it will be something to have efficiency back in the new kingdom.

3:19

[z]In the sweat of your face you shall eat bread Till you return to the ground, For out of it you were taken; [a]For dust you *are*, And to dust you shall return." Every time he worked, he was reminded that he was going to die because he sinned. No wonder

---

[t]1 Cor. 11:3; Eph. 5:22; 1 Tim. 2:12, 15
[u]1 Sam. 15:23
[v]Gen. 2:17
[w]Rom. 8:20–22; Heb. 6:8
[z]2 Thess. 3:10
[a]Gen. 2:7

we needed hope!

3:21

Also for Adam and his wife the LORD **God made tunics of skin,** since 1:31, God has not **made** anything. This is a skillful play on the word "done" in 3:13 ("what have you done/made"?) as they are the same Hebrew word. God, then, "did" this covering in response to the poor choice of Eve. **and clothed them.** God says "I didn't make this (what Eve did), but I'll make again because I love my creation."

The fact that **God made tunics of skin** implies that something died. Abel learned it, after all, from somebody (presumably Adam). Adam, in turn, learned it from somebody.

When we read the book of Revelation we become aware that generally everything is restored to this Edenic state. Yet, one thing that is not the same is that those in Revelation "walking with Jesus" have white raiment (Revelation 3:4-5; 16:15). There will be a testament of the fall and restoration forever. The same can be said in that our Savior has a glorified body that seems so dissimilar from the body that was buried in the tomb…except that He retains His scars. In the glorified world, then, it seems that the only tokens of the former life will be those of a redemption.

3:22-24[33]

24 So He drove out the man; and He placed cherubim at the east of the garden of Eden, Imagine the painful reminders— assuming that they may have checked the door to see if they could approach the tree of life.

---

[33]See also under 21:33.

Chapter 4

Now Adam knew Eve his wife, Did Adam sin by disregarding God's command to multiply? After all, the first mention of a child is not until Genesis chapter 4? The answer is "no." Looking at Genesis 1:27, the text states that male and female are created in God's image on the same day. Keeping in mind that Moses is writing this in retrospect, one should look ahead to 2:15-20. Still on Day 6, Adam is in the garden and given yet another command: He must name the animals. In verse 18, God says "I will make" which means Eve was not yet there at that time on day 6. In the timeline of Day 6, God brings the animals to Adam for naming (2:19-20), and then he is put to sleep, still on Day 6. By the end of Day 6, all the animals have been created and named, Adam was made from the ground and Eve was formed from Adam's side. Immediate obedience to "multiply" would not have been possible until Eve was made.

Was Eve's curse part of this command? Again the answer is "no." Looking at 3:16, God tells Eve that her sorrow (labor) and conception (pregnancy) will be multiplied, or made great. Therefore, Eve would have previously had the physical capability of labor and pregnancy. Chapter 3 is likely to have come very close in time after chapter 2; since she is not surprised at all by a talking serpent (and since delayed obedience of the command to multiply would have been disobedience and they had yet no children).

and she conceived and bore Cain, and said, "I have acquired a man from the LORD." She may have been thinking this was the fulfillment of God's promise in 3:15. **2 Then she bore again, this time his brother Abel. Now Abel was a keeper of sheep,** maybe

---

[34]See under 2:1-3 as well.

because he saw how necessary they were for sacrifice (3:21)? Leviticus 17:11 later informs the reader that God has an economy requiring bloodshed for sin.

but Cain was a tiller of the ground. Probably also learned from his parents. Adam was quite the worker of the ground. **3 And in the process of time it came to pass that Cain brought an offering of the fruit of the ground to the LORD.** This is often allowed, but not if this was an offering for the soul (Leviticus has many such offerings). **4 Abel also brought of the firstborn of his flock and of their fat. And the LORD respected Abel and his offering,** Hebrews 11:4 tells us why: **Abel** offered his offering "by faith." It could be, given Genesis 3:21, 4:7, and Leviticus 17:11, that this has a contextual flow leading us to Cain's faithless sacrifice being the wrong substance because he was of no such faith. Where did the boys receive the proper instruction? Well, we have to assume their parents taught them. When would they have taught them? On the occasion of sacrifices for their sins, and on these occasions, perhaps, the animals' skins would have been used as they were when God provided them in the garden for their parents.[35]

4:6-7

7 If you do well, will you not be accepted? The word here carries the idea of being "lifted." Psalm 3 says that God is the "lifter of our head." **And if you do not do well, sin lies at the door. And its desire *is* for you,** much like Eve's desire is for her husband— she wishes to usurp his authority—probably out of a fear of being dominated.

4:8

---

[35]With beautiful simplicity, a 19-year old (Dylan) in my small group at SRBC said, "Well, I'm sure Abel needed clothes too." Why didn't I think about that?

Now Cain talked with Abel his brother; and it came to pass, when they were in the field, that Cain rose up against Abel his brother and killed him. Matthew 23:35 puts the religious authorities of his day in Cain and He also calls Abel "righteous" and a "prophet" (Matthew 24:31).[36]

4:9

Then the LORD said to Cain, twice, now, God speaks to Cain whereas we find no record of His speaking to Abel.

4:10-11

And He said, "What have you done? The voice of your brother's blood cries out to Me from the ground. This makes the blood of Christ that "speaks better things than that of Abel" of great interest (Hebrews 12).[37] **11 So now you *are* cursed from the earth, which has opened its mouth to receive your brother's blood from your hand.** The earth is having a reaction to the blood? This sounds much like Romans 8:20-22 where the earth responds to sin. Leviticus 18:22 say much the same.

4:13-14

And Cain said to the LORD, "My punishment This is the only time in Genesis that this word is not translated "iniquity." *is* **greater than I can bear!** Even these 2500 years before the law of Moses.

4:16-18

---

[36]We find out from 2 Peter that Noah was a preacher, and we find out from Jude that Enoch was a prophet.

[37]Romans 3:25, meanwhile, says that Christ was sent to be our mercy seat, whereupon His blood was offered.

Then Cain went out from the presence of the LORD only Satan (Job 1-2) and Jonah (Jonah 1:2-3) are the only other personalities in Scripture that are described this way. **and dwelt in the land of [9]Nod on the east of Eden.** I wish this meant that **Cain** repented, but Jude 11 seems to tell us (based on Jude 19) that he died unrepentant.

17 And Cain knew his wife, So…where did Cain get his wife? [38] Answer: Cain married his older sister or younger niece. Eve could have given birth to multiples, or had only girls. Eve says in Genesis 4:1 "I've gotten an *ish* (Hebrew for man) from the Lord." Remembering the promise; Eve is delighted, she now has a son. This joy could be because after having only females, she now has an *ish.* Some theologians believe that pre-flood man developed faster, allowing Eve to reproduce faster. The Bible is silent about all these proposed children. Moses' focus in his Genesis chronicle was not the "many children Adam and Eve may have had;" nor was "how the first city developed" in his view. The purpose was to show the beginning of all things. Cain's wife would have been a sister or niece. Working backwards, from 5:3, Adam was 130 when he had Seth, as well as others, 33 boys and 23 girls according to Josephus.[39] Seth replaces Abel. It is likely that Abel was murdered near Seth's birth. If the fall happened the first year, there is almost 100 years of birth to explain the city's population.

Adam was commanded to multiply, name the animals, and then was given Eve. Before Eve's firstborn, the fall of Genesis 3 occurs. The couple was put out of the garden and their first child was born in sin. This "first child" or any of the supposed "23 girls" would have been a viable candidate for Cain's wife. Moreover, the seemingly expansive population of the city Cain built could have

---

[9] Lit. *Wandering*
[38] Researched and written by Brian Howell; Researched and Edited by Pastor Bill Sturm; Reviewed by Dr. Steve Wilson and Pastor Jonathan Andrews
[39] Whiston, William [translator]. *The Works of Josephus*. Hendrickson Publishers [First AD 93, this ed.1804] Book 1, Chapter 2, verse 3 footnote.

been any of Cain's older siblings and their offspring—already, at this point, in their 2nd and 3rd generation. Any of these nieces would have made a suitable wife.

Chapter 5

5:1-5[40]

These genealogies (here and chapter 11) serve to help us see that getting information from Adam to Jacob took a mere three "hand offs." **5 So all the days that Adam lived were nine hundred and thirty years; and he died.** This is why we think we can count the years to the creation of Adam, and therefore, creation. Genealogies such as here, Genesis 10 and Genesis 11 record the length of these lives and therefore, take us all the way to the life of Abraham.

5:21-27

24 And Enoch walked with God; This man was apparently the only person who could be thusly described since Adam (6 generations earlier, Jude 14).

5:32

And Noah was five hundred years old, and Noah begot Shem, Ham, and Japheth. This is the first time in this chapter where more than one child is named. Moses wanted the reader to know about a certain son from each father until now.

We have **Noah**'s children covered in chapter 10 (10:2, Japheth; 10:6, Ham; 10:21, Shem). Two full chapters, then, are completely comprised of genealogy. Chapter 11 ends with genealogy getting us to Abraham. Chapter 5 gets us to **Noah** and chapter 11 to Abraham. If one were to take out but two simple stories—**Noah** and the ark and the Tower of Babel—the body of Scripture would be an almost seem-less genealogy giving us the path of Adam to Abraham.

---

[40]See also under 2:15-17.

Of course, the section in chapter 11, shows us the narrowing of focus for the reader of Scripture from the human race to one of **Noah**'s sons. I don't want to quickly skirt the reality that mostly everyone died in the flood.

The "and he died" statement regarding **Noah** occurs in 10:28, proving this is essentially one passage with the interruptions of the flood and the tower of Babel. We are, without question, seeing the quaking reality that life is full of the reality of death now...thanks to Genesis 3. Genesis 2:17 promised this.

Chapter 6

And it came to pass, when men began to multiply on the face of the earth, and daughters were born unto them... That the sons of God saw the daughters of men that they were fair. "Who are the sons of God?" We have three possibilities here, really.

1. First of all, people have said that the sons of God were the good guys. Those we the people from the line of Seth. And the daughters of men were the women from the line of Cain. So, in other words, Cain and Seth were supposed to keep separate. These are the line of Seth and the line of Cain intermingling and it made God angry and so he bought a flood, because the truth is whatever takes place here is what brings the flood.

So something horrible happened here. And it is interesting that it is important that you see this because it is right in the middle of the genealogy. Now you have a promise early in the book of Genesis, you are expecting the fulfillment of Genesis 3:15. Here we are two or three chapters later and we have genealogy and then right in the middle of the genealogy we have this problem that deals with a race of people and another race of people or ethnicity or group or something that differentiates between **sons of God** and **daughters of men**. Now what is it? We don't know, but they produce, probably, from verse three, **giants, men of renowned**. It is apparently the tip top thing that brought the flood, and it has to do with reproduction. They had giants.

With this view no "daughters from Seth" and no "sons from Cain" intermingled. Isn't that what it would be saying? Because if that is what it was that would mean all the **sons** came from Seth and all the **daughters** came from Cain, is that where the **giants** came from?

2. The second possibility is that the sons of God is a ruling class,

kind of short hand for "kings who were in charge." Ok, well, then that means kings were marrying peasant girls, but that is it and they produced giants, ok? How could that be?

3. What was the first book written probably from the Bible? Job. And yet Genesis describes what happened first. So we should expect the writing styles of Genesis and Job to be a lot alike, right? We should expect to see a lot of the language used in Genesis that we see used in Job because although Genesis was written probably a long time after Job, Genesis describes what happened back in the time of Job.

We should see some similar language. And so there is as lot of things here that lead us to believe Job was not only the first book written, but it describes a time when the patriarchs lived on the earth.

> *Job 1:6 Now there was a day when **the sons of God** came to present themselves before the LORD, and Satan came also among them. And the LORD said unto Satan, Whence comest thou?*

It is most natural, then—if we have no other Scripture, to assume Satan—as an angel—is coming with other angels. If that is all we have, angels are in a sense **sons of God**.

> *Job 2:1 Again there was a day when **the sons of God** came to present themselves before the*
> *LORD, and Satan came also among them.*

Ok, so we have another day some time in distant past when sons of God came before the Lord and Satan was among them. Again, the natural idea here is that you have a bunch of angels coming and Satan is one of them. All right. So let's see if we can inform our guess work a little better here.

41

*Job 38:1-6 Then the LORD answered Job out of the whirlwind, and said, Who is this that darkeneth counsel by words without knowledge? Gird up now thy loins like a man; for I will demand of thee, and answer thou me. Where wast thou when I laid the foundations of the earth? declare, if thou hast understanding. Who hath laid the measures thereof, if thou knowest? or who hath stretched the line upon it? Whereupon are the foundations thereof fastened? 7. When the morning stars sang together, and all **the sons of God shouted for joy**?*

When were these **sons of God** shouting for joy if you take it with verse six? When the earth was created. So I don't know anyone else that was around back then other than angels. We are letting the Bible share with us what it means and we are going to adjust what we think according to Scripture, because that is what Bible believers do. But what God makes clear to Job here is that when he was laying the foundations, the **sons of God**, were shouting for joy. I have written more on my commentary on Job (1:6).

6:1b-2

And it came to pass, when men began to multiply on the face of the earth, and daughters were born unto them the sons of God who were probably angels **saw the daughters of men** the "and **daughters**" of chapter 5, it seems. Now the word there behind **saw** is this gazing desire. So you have men who are now looking at women and finding a particular class of men are looking at a particular class of women and finding them to be amazingly beautiful.

that they were fair. So they have the ability to be attracted to women. Did you get that idea there?

6:2b-4[41]

42

they took them wives of all which they chose. And the LORD said, My spirit shall not always strive with man, for that he also is flesh: yet his days shall be an hundred and twenty years. This seems like the amount of time between this pronouncement and the flood. With 5:32, this means Noah was about 480 years old when he started on the ark (he went into the ark, says chapter 7, in his 600ᵗʰ year).

There were giants If these were the result of those relationships discussed in the next phrase then we are talking about beings that are god-like or something? It may explain some sort of trace of a superior people who were not totally human. This may explain things like ancient maps before aircraft and before Antarctica had frozen over.[42] **in the earth in those days; and also after that, when the sons of God came in unto the daughters of men, and they bare children to them, the same became mighty men which were of old, men of renown.** It appears that these are angels who left the realm of being spirit beings possessed certain men, had weird unions with women and there came a genetically-altered race. This is not found anywhere else in Scripture other than in Numbers 13:33. Apparently, they made it through the flood (presumably genetically in one of the wives of Noah's sons).

What does **of old** mean? Now where have we seen that language before, of old? Micah 5:2 speaks of being everlasting from the past.

Whatever these giants were, they have been around a long time. When I let Scripture interpret Scripture I am left with believing that there were angels that fell and did some really debauched things.

---

[41]See also under 21:33.

[42]http://www.collective-evolution.com/2015/02/24/500-year-old-map-was-discovered-that-shatters-the-official-history-of-the-planet/ [accessed 5/7/18].

What else would you expect from the New Testament?

> *1 Peter 3:18 For Christ also hath once suffered for sins, the just for the unjust, that he might bring us to God, being put to death in the flesh, but quickened by the Spirit: By which also **he went and preached unto the spirits in prison;** Which sometime were disobedient, when once the longsuffering of God waited in the days of Noah, while the ark was a preparing, wherein few, that is, eight souls were saved by water.*

So whoever these spirits are in this prison, they were disobedient before Noah's flood. It doesn't tell us what the spirits are. But one thing is certain. You don't find anywhere in Peter's writings or in any of the discussion surrounding Peter where "spirits" is used to describe people who just don't have a body. So there is a hint. So we have spirits in a particular prison that were put there around the time of Noah's flood.

Peter made a promise about false prophets (2 Peter 2:1-3). They are going to be judged, and he gives a proof (2 Peter 2:4). I don't know if you noticed that or not, but we have 2 references from Peter talking about angels (or spirits) and Noah.

Couldn't that just be one fall from heaven? I mean, couldn't that be talking about the fall that happened before man was tempted in the garden? It is very clear at the time of Peter's writing, since he cast some devils out that they weren't all in hell. So we are not talking about all the angels here being thrown out of heaven as some kind of pre-human fall from heaven like the Isaiah 14 Lucifer falling from heaven. That can't be it, because not all the angels that sinned in that case are in hell. Some are still not in hell. Some of those demons are still alive on planet earth. So we are talking about a particular time when there was a particular sin that particular angels did and because of that they were put into a particular place. And it was sometime around Noah's flood.

"Hell" comes from three different Greek words in the New Testament. Remember, the Bible wasn't written in old English: *Hades* (*Sheol* is Hebrew); *Gahenna. Tartarus* is the one mentioned here and only mentioned here. This is the only time it is used in the entire New Testament. So there is a particular time and a particular place where particular angels were put after they did a particular sin. And it was around the time of Noah, we see in verse five.

> *Jude 6 And the angels which kept not their first estate, but left their own habitation, he hath reserved in everlasting chains under darkness unto the judgment of the great day.*

Ok, so we have angels that did a particular sin and you are like, "well, I don't really see a Noah thing happening here."

I think it is implied.

> *Jude 7 Even as Sodom and Gomorrha, and the cities about them **in like manner**, giving themselves over to fornication, and going after strange flesh, are set forth for an example, suffering the vengeance of eternal fire.*

Now ask yourself "Who indulged in sexual immorality?" The angels did, because Sodom and Gomorrah did it "likewise."

So we find in verse seven they partook of something that was sexually immoral, in my humble opinion, caused the flood. So we have three references here pointing to particular angels that left their first estate or left the realm of spirit only and came into the realm of humanity, probably possessed certain men, had intercourse with women, had a genetically altered race and God wanted to crush that particular offspring and did so in the flood. See more in my commentary on Revelation (9:1).

6:5-8

Then the LORD saw The "sons of god" **saw** (6:2), and the author wants you to draw the connection between what the "sons of god" **saw** and what the **LORD saw.** This connection is that God's actions are related to the sin of the "sons of god." Furthermore, verses 11 and 12 show that the corruption of the earth is related to the **evil** of **man.** What was this **evil** of **man?** It was at least sexual sin. May we remind ourselves to what degree God hates sin. Here Spurgeon for a refresher:

> Before I thought upon my soul's salvation, I dreamed that my sins were very few. All my sins were dead, as I imagined, and buried in the graveyard of forgetfulness. But that trumpet of conviction, which aroused my soul to think of eternal things, sounded a resurrectionnote to all my sins; and, oh, how they rose up in multitudes more countless then the sands of the sea! Now, I saw that my very thoughts were enough to damn me, that my words would sink me lower than the lowest hell; and as for my acts of sin, they now began to be a stench in my nostrils, so that I could not bear them. I thought I had rather have been a frog or a toad than have been made a man; I reckoned that the most defiled creature, the most loathsome and contemptible, was a better thing than myself, for I had so grossly and grievously sinned against Almighty God.[43]

6 And the LORD was sorry He was happy with what He did (1:31) and now He has a sort of sorrow about day six of Creation week. God was emotionally involved with His correction of His Creation.

---

[43] C. H. Spurgeon, *C. H. Spurgeon's Autobiography, Compiled from His Diary, Letters, and Records, by His Wife and His Private Secretary, 1834–1854*, vol. 1 (Cincinatti; Chicago; St. Louis: Curts & Jennings, 1898), 80–81.

God was equally affected when He saw Noah [6:8; 7:1 (same word "saw" is used in 7:1)].

All addictions, even sexual addictions, are idolatry. In 1 Kings 18 the question was "who will you worship" while the Ten Commandments begins with idolatry. So in the moment of bowing to one's addictions, a person is faced with whether they will worship the Lord or not. "Idolatry is anything that places anything above the worship of the Lord; anything that we place our affections upon that are greater than us than Jesus Christ."[44]

8 But Noah the historicity of this man is established in the previous chapter's genealogy: If he is not historical neither are the others in chapter 5. Of course there are others who mention Noah as a historical figure (Isaiah 54:9; Ezekiel 14:14-20; Matthew 24:37; Hebrews 11:7; 1 Peter 3:20; 2 Peter 2:4-5). The motive for discrediting his historicity is so that one might discount Adam's anti-type, Christ (see Paul's discussion comparing the two in Romans 5 and 1 Corinthians 15).

found grace in the eyes of the LORD. It seems as though his dad thought **Noah** would be special (5:28). On the other hand, maybe everybody thought that (4:1). This phrase definitely means that while the world of mankind made God sorry; **Noah** made him happy (see 7:1 also). This sort of leads the reader to see **Noah** seeing the **LORD's eyes**. After all, we recently read, in chapter 4, that Cain's face was fallen. In other words, there was no face to face contact with God. Cain found no approval in God's **eyes** while Noah did. **Noah** sees a kinder demeanor than did Cain and his children. It seems that this is the message of Moses.

6:9-10

---

[44]approximately 9:00 into this seminar: http://t4g.org/media/2018/04/what-is-addiction/ [accessed 8/7/18].

This is the genealogy of Noah. Noah was a just man, [6]perfect in his generations. Noah walked with God. As Enoch did.

It is worthy of note that **Noah** finds no ability, it seems, to **walk with God** if he did not first find grace in God's eyes (6:8). **10 And Noah begot three sons: [o]Shem, Ham, and Japheth.** He is 500 years old (5:32) at this point and thought it seems that the ark begun immediately upon God's pronouncement in 6:3 thus making **Noah** 480 years old, we are not entirely sure, based on the chronology between this verse and God's words in verse 13 that the ark didn't begin until after the boys were born.

6:13-21

And God said to Noah, "The end of all flesh has come before Me, nobody reads this as it is and thinks, "I'll bet this is a local flood in just the Mesopotamian Valley." No, you have to assume that Moses meant something different than what he wrote or that his writings were corrupted. This view of local flood, then, is akin to "old earth" theory because if there is no universal flood, then you need another explanation for world-wide discovery of fossils. **for the earth is filled with violence** This may have had something to do with Cain (chapter 4) or with the *nephilim.* However, 9:6 tells us that God wanted this dealt with post-Flood with great expedience.

through them; and behold, I will destroy them with the earth. If this were nothing but a local Flood, it seems superfluous to spend years and years building an ark when they could have simply moved out of the region. Other questions like "why make a covenant with a bow (chapter 9) to "never again flood the earth" if we are simply talking about a regional flood? **14 Make yourself an ark** since this is the same word used in the **ark** in which Moses

---

[6]blameless or *having integrity*
[o]Gen. 5:32

was hidden,[45] we see that it is more of a box/container rather than a modern understanding of "boat."[46]

15 And this is how you shall make it: The length of the ark *shall be* **three hundred cubits,** The most conservative **cubit** known from this time is about 18 inches. It is probable that this was the average length of the tip of the center finger to the elbow.

its width fifty cubits, and its height thirty cubits. This is roughly 1,500,000 cubic feet of space. This is roughly the carrying capacity of over 560 standard railroad boxcars providing space for more than 50,000 animals approximately the size of a sheep or smaller,[47] leaving more than ½ the space for living quarters and provisions.[48]

16 You shall make a window for the ark, and you shall finish it to a cubit from above; 8:13 leads me to believe this was a simple window as literally as this sounds.

17 And behold, I Myself am bringing ˣfloodwaters on the earth, to destroy from under heaven all flesh in which *is* **the breath of life;** these animals, then, have lungs. We don't have to have any other type on the ark in our understanding. Genesis 2:18-19 show us that these animals came out of the ground just like mankind (2:7). What makes these animals different from mankind, then? They are not made in the image of God (1:26-27).

18 But I will establish My covenant with you; 9:11 shows us this was a covenant with all the "living creatures" on the ark as well,

---

[45]the **ark** of the Covenant is a different word.

[46]Both Noah and Moses were saved by water [so is the believer…in a way (1 Peter 3:21)].

[47]While some are grossly larger than a sheep, many are much smaller (a beaver, for example).

[48]This data is provided by my friend, Adam Greene of Berean Baptist Church, Fayetteville, NC.

ˣ2 Pet. 3:6

and the substance of the **covenant** is that God would never flood the earth again. **and you shall go into the ark—you, your sons, your wife, and your sons' wives with you.** 8 of them (2 Peter 2:5). **19 And of every living thing of all flesh you shall bring two of every** *sort* **into the ark,** these came of their own accord, it seems (verse 20). There is no need to assume that these animals had to come from furthest extents of the earth. Job 22 speaks of the Flood as past. Therefore, those animals described (even the dinosaur) in Job 38-41 were on **the ark** (assuming they had lungs, and it seems as though they did).

6:22

Thus Noah did; according to all that God commanded him, according to chapter 7 as well.

Chapter 7

7:1-6[49]

Then the LORD said to Noah, "Come this word can mean "go" as well, but 8:16 has a word that can only mean "go" which means that here **come** is the correct translation. This means that God is in the **ark** with His people.

7:7-12

10 And it came to pass after seven days taken with verse 13 it seems that there was another week before Noah and his family went into the ark. Luke 17:27 removes all doubt to this.

11 In the six hundredth year of Noah's life, in the second month, the seventeenth day of the month, They disembark a year and ten days later (8:14)

on that day all the fountains of the great deep were broken up, this explains how we have fossils on the top of mountain ranges.

7:17-24

And the waters prevailed on the earth one hundred and fifty days. 7:19-20 give us this in different terms while 8:3 gives it to us in these terms again.

---

[49]See also under 2:1-3.

51

Chapter 8

Then God remembered Noah, We know **God** does not forget in a literal sense so this must have a cognitive intent attached to its usage. God, then, doesn't really "forget our sin."[50] **and every living thing, and all the animals that** *were* **with him in the ark. And God made a wind to pass over the earth, and the waters subsided.** And this occurs until the time listed in 8:5. See a note on this great wind:

> The early phases…would have been quite violent. With nothing but a shoreless ocean, these winds would generate tremendous waves and currents, and vast quantities of water would be evaporated, especially in the equatorial regions.[51]

The biblical authors also give us a peek at this moment—perhaps creation week as well covered in 1:9 (Job 12:15; Psalm 104:6-9).

4 Then the ark rested in the seventh month, the seventeenth day of the month, So while this may not be the calendar Noah used, Moses' calendar says this was exactly 5 months after the water started (7:11) [lasting the first 40 days of the 150 days (7:12)] upon the entrance of the family into the ark (7:13), thus informing us that a month had 30 days in it on Moses' calendar (referencing the "150 days" of 8:3).

5 And the waters decreased continually until the tenth month. In the tenth *month,* **on the first** *day* **of the month,** It has been, then, 233 days since the rain started and 83 days for the waters to decrease to the point where **the tops of the mountains were seen.** They were, then, on one of the highest mountains. This is

---

[50]See my commentary on Hosea (8:13).
[51]Henry Morris *The Genesis Record*, 206.

obviously not a local flood.

8:6-12

So it came to pass, at the end of forty days, this is additional to 8:5 and we are then at 273 days.

12 So he waited yet another seven days and sent out the dove, which did not return again to him anymore. It seems that we are at about 287 days (9 months and 17 days) into the "flood."

8:13-14

And it came to pass in the six hundred and first year, in the first *month,* the first *day* of the month, Considering 7:11 & 8:4, this is 56 days before they left the ark (29 days left in the first month and 27 days of the 2nd month until they leave the ark). **that the waters were dried up from the earth; and Noah removed the covering of the ark** if God shut the door (7:16) then this must be the window above (discussed in 6:16).

Chapter 9

9:6-11[52]

"Whoever sheds man's blood, By man his blood shall be shed; [k]**F or in the image of God He made man.** The function of capital punishment is not to deter reconciliation or to restore peace to those left behind from the victim's family; rather, this is meant to be a deterrent to murder (Ecclesiastes 8:11; Romans 13:3-4). Some cultures have decided that their children should grow up with deterrence to murder.[53] Some have thought to make ethnic inequality an argument against capital punishment among murderers.[54] However, there is no need to argue this if the "discriminated party" doesn't murder.

James 3:9 reminds us, though marred, we are the **image of God,** and as such, it is heinous to kill a human being.

7 And as for you, be fruitful and multiply; Bring forth abundantly in the earth And multiply in it." God does not appear to be nervous about over population.

9 "And as for Me, behold, I establish My covenant with you and with your descendants after you, This is not two-parties. This is unilateral. It is carried on through verse 17.

11 Thus I establish My covenant with you: Never again shall all flesh be cut off by the waters of the flood; never again shall there be a flood to destroy the earth." This is another proof of a universal **flood,** rather than the liberal idea of a local **flood.**

---

[52]See also under 2:1-3.

[k]Gen. 1:26, 27

[53]https://www.memri.org/reports/criticism-iran-over-children-attending-public-executions [accessed 8/16/18].

[54] http://www.christianitytoday.com/women/2015/june/let-boston-bomber-live.html [accessed 8/6/18].

15 and I will remember My covenant God discussing His memory is mere **Covenant** language and, as in 8:1, implies intent to act. **which *is* between Me and you and every living creature of all flesh;** God did communicate with the animals, it seems (to get them to the ark), to a donkey (Numbers 23-24), to ravens (1 Kings 19), and to a great fish (Jonah 2). They were furthermore wrought from the ground (Genesis 2) and have the breath of life (Genesis 7); two significant similarities with mankind. They are, therefore, special, and as such—deemed worthy of a **covenant**.

the waters shall never again become a flood to destroy all flesh. Matthew 5:17, Matthew 24:35, 2 Peter 3:1-10, and Revelation 20:11-12 remind us that the earth will be destroyed again (while Hebrews 1:10-12 drive us to define what we mean), but it will never again happen with water.

16 everlasting covenant symbolized by a rainbow. We see this carrying forth to Colossians 1:20 where "all things" are "reconciled." In other words, as here, he has a **covenant** with all creation. Hebrews 13:20 speaks of this yet again where the blood of Christ secured this **everlasting covenant.** Revelation 4 & 5 speak of a rainbow being around the throne and elders and the four beasts. This is a Bible-wide drama. Again, see the table of Genesis/Revelation in my commentary on Revelation.

17 And God said to Noah, "This *is* the sign in the Septuagint, even, this is not the same Greek word as found in 2 Corinthians 1 or Ephesians 1 and the word "earnest" when referring to the believer's taste of glory in the Holy Spirit, but it may have the same application.

of the covenant while the perverts of today are endeavoring to

---

[55]See also under 21:33.

hijack the **rainbow**—to include the largest bank in America,[56] television networks,[57] metropolitan governments,[58] so-called evangelical preachers,[59] department stores,[60] numerous Fortune 500 companies,[61] and even the Department of Defense[62]—this is God's beautiful **sign.**

which I have established between Me and all flesh every human being came off the ark (Genesis 9:19; Acts 17:26). **that *is* on the earth."** Here, then, is the reality: the "rainbow" is not intended to remind us of a sinful lifestyle but of a loving God Who keeps His promises.

9:18-20

18 Now the sons of Noah who went out of the ark were Shem, Ham, and Japheth. And Ham *was* the father of Canaan. We are being prepped, as in verse 22, for the conquest of **Canaan.**

9:21-23[63]

[56]https://christiannews.net/2014/07/07/chilling-implications-largest-u-s-bank-asks-workers-if-they-support-homosexuality/ [accessed 8/13/18].

[57]https://www.christianpost.com/news/glaad-calls-on-ae-to-end-duck-dynasty-after-phil-robertson-calls-homosexuality-a-sin-111073/ [accessed 8/13/18].

[58]https://www.washingtontimes.com/news/2014/nov/25/atlanta-fire-chief-kelvin-cochran-suspended-for-ga/ [accessed 8/13/18].

[59]https://christiannews.net/2013/03/18/no-hell-bell-comes-out-in-support-of-homosexuality-tells-narrow-christians-to-repent/ [accessed 8/13/18].

[60]https://www.sermonaudio.com/sermoninfo.asp?SID=622121519494 [accessed 8/13/18].

[61]https://www.christianpost.com/news/google-facebook-amazon-among-200-businesses-filing-brief-supporting-gay-marriage-90897/ [accessed 8/13/18].

[62]https://www.sermonaudio.com/sermoninfo.asp?SID=82013107489 [accessed 8/13/18].

[63]See also under 38:1-5.

Then he drank of the wine and was drunk, whether he knew what it took to be drunk or whether it was even possible before the flood, we don't know. All we know is that this first mention of **wine** in the Bible is also the first mention of **drunk**enness. We'll see more of this in chapter 19 and we just know that if you see what appears to be the entire world dying…you may do some extreme things.

and became uncovered in his tent. Here is another similarity, then, between Adam and Noah: 1. Both fell through fruit; 2. Both walked with God; 3. Both had three sons; 4. Both lived over 900 years; 5. Cursing results (the ground; Ham); 6. Both are charged with populating the earth; 7. Both had animals brought to them; and here 8. Both were shamed in nakedness; 9. Somebody else covered them (coats of skins from God; Shem and Japheth).

22 And Ham, the father of Canaan, saw the nakedness of his father, and told his two brothers outside. Since, in that Genesis 19 passage children got their father drunk to "see his nakedness", it seems like that could be the case here.

23 But Shem and Japheth 5:32 tells us Noah was around 500 years old when the boys were born and the flood came when Noah was 600. These boys were 100 years old. They were not the same age exactly, as is seen in verse 24 [Shem was 98 at the flood (11:10) which means he was probably the middle child while Ham was the youngest (verse 24)].

9:24-27

So Noah awoke from his wine, and knew what his younger son had done to him. At the very least, he embarrassed his father; at the very most, something sexual took place (consider the parallel passage in Genesis 19 where incest took place from wine).
25 Then he said: "Cursed *be* **Canaan;** So Ham is not **cursed,** but rather Ham's youngest son, it seems, is **cursed.** Perhaps it is

because he took part with Ham's sin; perhaps it is because Ham is Abraham's youngest son.

Here is God's dictate for the general genocide of these people. **A servant of servants He shall be to his brethren."** The conquest of **Canaan** has something to do with this **curs**ing. There are approximately 400 years between this cursing and the settling of Abraham in **Canaan. 26 And he said: "Blessed** *be* **the LORD, The God of Shem, And may Canaan be his** the descendants of **Canaan** served the descendants of **Shem** in their own lands not far away.

servant. This, from the perspective of the author who was to lead the children of Israel to **Canaan** (Exodus 3), makes the development of this story necessary beginning here in Genesis.

27 May God enlarge Japheth, And may he dwell in the tents of Shem; Psalm 84:10 seems to interpret this as a way of taking part in another person's inheritance. So, **Japheth** will share the inheritance of **Shem** as stipulated in Genesis 12:1-3 and Galatians 3:8. This reality was first seen when the Europeans heard the Gospel from the fallout of Pentecost (Acts 2) and then later when Paul came to Europe in Acts 16.

Chapter 10

10:1

Now this *is* the genealogy after Genesis 5, we pick up where that left off. It is as if we have a **genealogy** that is one branch thick to get us to **Noah,** and now it picks back up after four chapters of the Flood account with the three branches of **Noah**'s family.

10:2-5

The sons of Japheth the first of three sons (10:6 & 10:22).

5 From these the coastland *peoples* of the Gentiles were separated into their lands, everyone according to his language, according to their families, into their nations. This seems to be the first of three Tower of Babel mentions in this chapter (11:1-9).

10:6-7

The sons of Ham the second of three sons (10:2 & 10:22), and 9:24 leads me to believe **Ham** is the youngest.

10:10-12

And the beginning of his kingdom was Babel, Erech, Accad, and Calneh, in the land of Shinar. It appears, then, based on this reference and 10:30 that at least two of three of Noah's sons were involved at the Tower of Babel.

10:21-22

And *children* were born also to Shem, the father of all the children of Eber, the brother of Japheth the elder.[64] 11:10

---

[64]Some alternate versions say **Shem** was **the elder.** Of course, they cannot both be correct. 1. The first son was born to Noah at 500 (Genesis 5:32).

59

proves they were not merely triplets. There were two years between these boys.

22 The sons of Shem This is the 3rd of three sons (10:2; 10:6) *were* **Elam, Asshur, Arphaxad,** This is where our genealogy picks back up in 11:10 to get us to Abraham in order for the rest of the book to focus on one man's family, and the reader knows the promise, now, of a seed to crush the serpent (3:15).

10:25-30

To Eber were born two sons: the name of one *was* **7Peleg, for in his days the earth was divided;** This seems like the 2nd of three Babel mentions in this chapter. It is hard to tell whether he received this name to prophesy of it or whether he received this name proleptically by Moses (as is discussed throughout this commentary.

30 And their dwelling place was from Mesha as you go toward Sephar, the mountain of the east. It seems like we are being told this because of their part in the next chapter (11:2).

10:32

These *were* **the families of the sons of Noah, according to their generations, in their nations; and from these the nations were**

The Flood came in Noah's 600th birthday (Genesis 7:11). That means at least one of Noah's sons was older than Shem, who was 98 at the flood (Genesis 11:10). Either it was Japheth or it was Ham. If it was possibly Japheth, then maybe the newer Bibles (with their underlying Hebrew from which they are translated) are correct. 2. Ham was known as the "younger son" (Gen 9:24). Oddly enough, of the other 19 times this "younger" is used in Genesis, 18 of them are clearly referring to the "youngest" rather than merely "younger". If Ham is the youngest, that means he was younger than Shem. 3. Therefore, if one of the boys was 100 at the time of the flood; and Shem was 98 at the flood; and Ham is the youngest, then clearly **Japheth** must be **the elder.**

7 Lit. *Division*

divided here is, apparently, the 3rd of three Tower of Babel mentions in chapter 10. We might be thinking "how did this **divid**ing occur?" Moses breaks from the genealogy in the next chapter to answer this before returning to show us how Abraham got here.

Chapter 11

11:1-4

Now the whole earth had one language and one speech.
Looking at 10:5, we see that this will soon change in this current
narrative. We will now read how it was "divided." **2 And it came
to pass, as they journeyed from the east, that they found a
plain in the land of Shinar, and they dwelt there.** When you
consider Revelation 5:9-10, Revelation 13:8, and the speaking of
"healing of the nations" in the later part of Revelation 21 and the
beginning of Revelation 22, you see that this Bible is really about
one book.[65]

4 And they said, "Come, let us countered by the Godhead's **let us**
in 11:7.

build ourselves a city, This is rebellion since Noah was given a
mandate to refurbish the earth (9:1-2). **and a tower whose top** *is*
in the heavens; Deuteronomy 1:28 & 9:1 shows that this can be a
figure of speech to simply mean something of great height. Since
Moses wrote both books it seems acceptable that both meant
simply "immense height." Also, don't forget that the **heavens** were
low enough for the birds to be in them (Genesis 1:20). In other
words, the **tower** would be tall enough that they were "up there
with the birds."

let us make a name for ourselves, "Let people talk about us
forever." **lest we be scattered abroad over the face of the whole
earth."** They may have had a morbid fear of another flood and
being forgotten—thus the tower to counter the rising waters.

11:5-9

---

[65]See my table on Revelation and Genesis at the beginning of my
commentary on Revelation.

But the LORD **came down** ironic, isn't it? The tower is to reach to the heavens, and God has to crouch **down to see the city** Exodus 3:8 shows us that when God "goes down" it is in the form of the Angel of the **LORD.** Probably, then, the **LORD** who looks like a man with two angels in Genesis 18-19 is the Angel of the **LORD,** and is probably the "us" of 11:7.

6 And the LORD **said, "Indeed** ᶠ**the people** *are* **one and they all have one language,** and will be again one day (Zephaniah 3:8). **and this is what they begin to do; now nothing that they** ʰ**propo se to do will be withheld from them.** It could be that God is intervening so that He doesn't have to destroy this people again as in the flood (6:5). **7 Come, let Us** As an alternative view, it could be that this is used in the same way as in 1:26. Since mankind is not made in the image of angels (1:26-27) we should probably assume the **us** is not angels but the more than one Person that are the **LORD.**

Go down is a wee bit humorous for it plays on the desire of the people to build a tower to reach up (11:4). They are striving to reach up while God must work to crouch down to see their silly tower. Oddly enough, God not only has to "humble Himself" to see the earth, He actually has to bend His knees slightly to see the Heavens (Psalm 113:6). Of course I am speaking anthropologically.

8 So the LORD **scattered them abroad** if we think about it, social media is now a virtual tower of Babel where ideas are gathered and crowd dynamics are stirred up instantly.[66] People don't even need to move or actually gather. They can do things with less thought than ever before.

ᶠGen. 9:19; Acts 17:26

ʰPs. 2:1

[66]https://www.christianpost.com/news/christian-apologist-says-social-media-like-the-tower-of-babel-93149/ [accessed 8/16/18].

11:10-11

This *is* the genealogy of Shem: Shem *was* one hundred years old, and begot Arphaxad two years after the flood. This means, frankly, that **Shem** was 97 years old (at least) when he was on the ark during the **flood.** This means that the Pearl of Great Price, a piece of Mormon "Scripture" is mistaken when it says—at least as late as the 1976 version—that that Shem was born in Noah's 493rd year (Moses 8:12). Genesis 7:6 says the **Flood** came in Noah's 601st year. According to this Pearl of Great Price reference, **Shem,** being born when Noah was 493 was actually 107 years old rather than the true Biblical age of 98 years old.

11:31

And Terah took his son Abram and his grandson Lot, the son of Haran, and his daughter-in-law Sarai, his son Abram's wife, and they went out with them from So, **Abram** didn't leave alone. He actually went with his father to **Canaan. Terah** died in **Canaan.**

Chapter 12

Now the LORD had said It seems, then, that this calling came before 11:31. Nehemiah (Nehemiah 9) and Stephen (Acts 7) both say **Abram** was called out of the "Ur of the Chaldeans." It seems, then, that 12:1-4 are parenthetical.

"Get out of your country, From your family And from your father's house, If this really occurred before 11:31, did **Abram** partially disobey, having brought his **father's house** all the way to Canaan.

3 I will bless those who bless you, And I will curse him who curses you; And in you all the families of the earth shall be blessed." Does this mean that no matter what the people of Abraham do, they are God's chosen? Or, does it mean that the church of this dispensation replaced Israel? I say "no" and "no." I say that Christ is the fulfillment of this promise and that all those in Christ are recipients of this promise. Paul the Apostle heard the message of Stephen in Acts 7 and wrote, later as a Christian, to the Galatian believers. He said one Jew was in mind here in Genesis 12 and His Name is "Jesus" (Galatians 3:16). So all those nations (**families**) in Christ will be blessed. God does not have a "chosen people" outside of His Christ. So, all promises concerning the restoration of ethnic Israel (Jeremiah 33:25; Ezekiel 36-37; Romans 11) are because of their mass conversion to Christ.

Maybe we should also point out that this peculiarity that Abraham enjoys is because God wants to save the world:

> We sense immediately that the God who would speak such words is no petty tribal god. He is a God whose plans are both benign and universal, spanning all ages and cultures.

---

[67]See also under 1:26-28.

If He retaliates against enemies of Abraham, it is not just to protect Abraham, but to keep the enemies from extinguishing a fire kindled to warm the whole world.[68]

12:4-6[69]

So Abram departed as the LORD had spoken to him, and Lot went with him. And Abram *was* seventy-five years old when he departed from Haran. Galatians 3:17 seems to place this at the beginning of the 430-year countdown to the Exodus (Exodus 12:40).[70] 1 Kings 6:1 places 480 years after the Exodus into the fourth year of Solomon. Using, then, the genealogies of Genesis 5 and 11[71] we can see how many years after creation that Solomon built his temple. This account here occurs 2024 years after creation[72] (or 1852 BC, using 966 BC as the date for Solomon's temple).

6 Abram passed through the land to the place of Shechem, as far as the terebinth tree of Moreh. And the Canaanites *were* then in the land. He is a descendant of Ham (see chapter 9). We are being told they **were in the land** to prepare us for events later in Moses' writing.

12:7-9

Then the LORD appeared to Abram just as in Genesis 18:1. John 8:56-58 show us that this was probably Pre-incarnate Jesus.

12:10-13

---

[68]Don Richardson *Eternity in Their Hearts (Revised)* (Ventura, CA: Regal Books, 1981), 155.

[69]See also under the introduction.

[70]It could also be that this starts in Genesis 17:8 in Abram's 99th year. 24 years difference in the grand scheme isn't much.

[71]Some have wondered whether there were gaps in these genealogies. I say that the "year count" is Moses' way of being specific with the timeline, thus disallowing gaps.

[72]This comes with some assumptions (like that Abraham was a triplet).

Now there was a famine in the land, and Abram went down to Egypt close to a thousand people with Abraham with over 300 fighting men in his house in the next two chapters? This could be how they were noticed in their travels (12:15).

13 Please say you *are* my sister, This is the first time of two this happens with Abraham and Sarah (20:12) around 14 years later (given that Ishmael is born at Abraham's 87th year in Chapter 16 and Isaac is born in Abraham's 101st year in chapter 21), but we see in that verse that they are half siblings indeed. It is Leviticus 18 when this is prohibited and so we are a several hundred years before it was penned.

Isaac did, however, tell a lie when he adopted this scheme in Genesis 26. Rebekah was not his half sister. Furthermore, Lot's own morals are obviously skewed as he ends up with his daughters (Genesis 19). Did he learn that from uncle Abe?

Abraham did know the story of Adam and Eve. He should have known that it was his calling to protect his wife from the seat of temptation.

Chapter 13

13:1-2

2 Abram *was* very rich in livestock, in silver, and in gold. Partly because he gained from his indiscretion in Egypt, but mostly because God promised him increased blessing already. Hebrews 11 should tell us that "nothing outside the realm of faith is memorialized by God." Also, we could surmise that is it forgotten. Hebrews 11:17 even shows us that Isaac was counted as Abraham's first child, not Ishmael. Isaac was begotten by faith, and so the only one mentioned in Hebrews 11.

13:15[73]

---

[73]See under 21:33.

Chapter 14[74]

14:17

And the king of Sodom went out to meet him at the Valley of Shaveh (that *is,* the King's Valley), I really like what this author adds to the explanation of how this **king of** Salem (14:18) gets into this account: "perhaps the small plain where the Kidron, Hinnom, and Tyropoeon valleys come together, east of Jerusalem. This proximity to Jerusalem explains the sudden appearance of Melchizedek, the king of Salem (= Jerusalem)."[76] This little

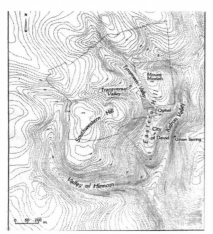

topographical sketch helps somewhat (I found it in the back of my Oxford Bible years ago).

14:18-19

Then Melchizedek king of Salem[77] brought out bread and wine; Here is a pre-Old Testament (as defined by Galatians 3:17) and pre-New Testament (as defined by Hebrews 9:17) communion service (as described in Luke 22:19-20) led by a man who pictured Jesus Christ (as described in Hebrews 7:1-10) before Abraham, who was not only the genetic Israel (as delineated in Hebrews 7:10), but was also the picture of the embryonic and Jewish church (as described in Luke 22:17-20 and defined in Ephesians 2:20)

---

[74]See under 2:1-3.

[75]See under introduction.

[76] K. A. Mathews, *Genesis 11:27–50:26*, vol. 1B, The New American Commentary (Nashville: Broadman & Holman Publishers, 2005), 148.

[77]See the topographical map of Jeru**salem** which was discovered in the back of my Oxford Bible.

because of genetics and because of His calling "from out" his father's house (Genesis 12:1-3).[78]

So, since we have all of these pre-Old Testament things in this story we should find it to be no surprise that we also find a pre-New Testament reality in the Lord's Supper here. However, and this disappoints me to be sure, there are a great many references to "bread and wine" in the Old Testament and I feel a little bit out of line to make only this occurrence significant in this regard. In other words, it seems as though it is a shorthand for "manifold provisions."[79] However, if Christ is present in Melchizedek and the church is present in Abraham, then I feel license to see here the Lord's Supper.

1. Christ met with His disciples. (Luke 22:7-20)
2. Christ meets with His disciples. When all else seems like it is being removed from you, never forget in this meeting around the Lord's table, Christ will not be removed from you. Christ will never again be taken from you.

3. Christ will meet with His disciples (Genesis 14:17; 14:20; Luke 22:16; 22:18). After the enemies are dead and when we sit again; again in the kingdom.

14:20[80]

And blessed be God Most High, We know this is not a theophany because this man rather **blesses God. Who has delivered your enemies into your hand."** Indeed, this was miraculous, given the defeating of four kings (14:1; 14:9) with 318 men (14:14).

---

[78]See my commentary on Matthew (footnote on 16:18).
[79]"KJV Search Results for "h3899" AND "h3196"." Blue Letter Bible. Web. 26 Mar, 2019.
<https://www.blueletterbible.org//search/search.cfm?Criteria=h3899+h3196&t=KJV#s=s_primary_0_1>.
[80]See under 2:1-3 & 28:18-22 also.

Chapter 15

15:1-2

After these things the word of the LORD came to Abram Could this actually be a visage of the pre-incarnate Christ, the Word (John 1:14)? It seems it could be since "Abraham saw [Christ's] day" (John 8).[81]

2 But Abram said, "Lord GOD, what will You give me, seeing I go childless, and the heir of my house is Eliezer of Damascus?" "You've given me a lot, but to whom do I leave it?" Abraham is acknowledging that God made him wealthy [through inheritance from Terah (chapter 11), the trip to Egypt (chapter 12), and the spoiling of the kings (chapter 14)], and yet he has nobody to whom he may impart it. He's a little preoccupied with the whole thing because God gave he and his sons land and now he's going to give it to a Syrian?

In Exodus 18, we find Moses naming one of his sons Eliezer (actually born in Exodus 3). God did not identify Himself as "the God of Abraham" until this chapter. Eliezer is then born and named. Chapter 18 says he received this name because he was "saved from the sword of Pharaoh." Meanwhile Moses writes both Genesis and Exodus after his begetting and his naming of Eliezer—the 2nd Eliezer—after both Eliezers are born in households of separate men (Abraham & Moses) who were both delivered from Pharaoh (Genesis 12 and Exodus 13-14).

15:3

Then Abram said, "Look, You have given me no offspring; indeed one born in my house is my heir!" Genesis 22:1 speaks of Abraham being 100 years old when Isaac is born. The last verse of Genesis 16 says that Abram was 86 when Ishmael was born. Since

---

[81]If that Scripture was not fulfilled in Melchizedek (Genesis 14).

Ishmael is not yet born, Abram is not yet 86 years old, and this passage is no less than 14 years before Isaac is born.

We can understand Abram's concern with having an heir. He wants somebody to leave his riches with and to be recipients of the land after him (Genesis 12:7; 13:15-16). Abram is understandably puzzled. We know he is probably in his 80's and time seems to be running out.

15:4

And behold, the word of the LORD came to him, This is the 2nd time in four verses it says this and there are no other times in Genesis where it says this. By the way, Galatians 3 says "the Scripture testified." So Paul calls it "the Scripture" and Moses called it **the word of the LORD**. If what you have is "Scripture," it is also **the word of the LORD.** "Scripture" is the "spoken Word of God."

15:6

And he believed in the LORD, and He accounted it to him for righteousness. So what did Abraham believe? Galatians 3:8 says he believed "the Gospel" in this very instance. An Old Testament saint had to believe the Gospel to be saved. Nothing has changed. Somewhere, Abram believed the Gospel, and if it is a different Gospel than what we believe, then it was a "false Gospel." Look at Galatians 1:8-9 and see for yourself. Paul uses the same word two chapters from each other.

There were some weak-faith days for Abraham, but this was not it. Genesis 12 and Sarah? Sure. Here? No. There were many days of nothing amazing going on. He was doing normal things on normal days getting ready for "big days." Acts tells us this many different ways: "build tents and minister on Sabbath days." In regards to kingdom expansion, there was nothing significant occurring? Here,

72

we have lots of boring days where Abram is…simply being faith-filled.[82]

15:7

I am the LORD We should acknowledge that Exodus 6:1-3 helps us with a little light on this. Moses, the same author in both places is simply writing Genesis proleptically: Moses was the first person to hear God's name since Abraham, but used the name in the writing of this history involving Abraham.

This is like Genesis 47:11. Moses, who wrote both books, writes about Ramses before it existed in Genesis 47:11. Perhaps this is the best example of how this could work: I lived in 1945 and I wrote about my experience in 1965. All my readers have been born since 1945 and the town changed names in 1946. Which name do I use if I only want to use one? I would naturally use the name that I felt worked the best to bring clarity in the most concise manner: the name by which everybody knew the town in 1965. That is writing proleptically, and many skeptics (for some reason) don't allow for this at all.[83]

Otherwise, in its New Testament form, Genesis and Exodus were attributed to Moses by Jesus (Mark 12:26). That means that Moses wrote enough of both books to be known as the author—even if an editor later arrived and did some minute person/town name changes.

15:11

---

[82]More on Abraham's faithfulness here: http://www.sermonaudio.com/sermoninfo.asp?SID=12212201105 [accessed 12/29/16].

[83]See page 10: http://www.usislam.org/pdf/Jesus-interrupted-Bart-D-ehrman.pdf [accessed 10/19/18].

And when the vultures came down on the carcasses, Abram drove them away. A splendid mixture of the sovereignty of God and the responsibility of man: God shows up and makes a unilateral covenant—giving everything to Abram and his offspring…but Abram better keep the animals in tact until then.

15:15-21

Now as for you, you shall go to your fathers in peace; you shall be buried at a good old age. With all that he had been through, he still had roughly 90 years left in his life. **16 But in the fourth generation they shall return here, for the iniquity of the Amorites** Deuteronomy 3 singles out these two kings. They are east of the Jordan River so they are not even in what would become the "Promised Land." **is not yet complete."** It could be that these **Amorites** are so terrible that this is shorthand for all the people of Canaan (see more complete list in verses 19-21), but I think we can do better. Genesis 14:13 & 14:24 show us that it was an **Amorite** that had made a covenant with Abraham and this may have bought them some more years: safety from getting pummeled by Abraham. Abraham has even more of a relationship with them in his 100th year, it seems (18:1).

17 And it came to pass, when the sun went down and it was dark, that behold, there appeared a smoking oven and a burning torch that passed between those pieces. Two covenanting parties would walk between severed bodies, in that day, to say "if we break our covenant, may we be like unto these animals" (Jeremiah 34:18).[84] This is a unilateral covenant/promise which demonstrates God doing something without another party. Hebrews 6:13 speaks of God doing thing—swearing by Himself because there was no greater by which He could swear. This was a promise to Abraham's seed, we're told. Galatians 3:7 seems to put

---

[84]As if to say "the LORD to so to me and more also" as with Ruth towards Naomi (Ruth 1).

this promise to Abraham not only to seed…but to seed "in Christ": Jew or Gentile.

18 On the same day the LORD made a covenant with Abram, saying: "To your descendants I have given this land, from the river of Egypt to the great river, the River Euphrates—We see that the Promised Land, then, goes way eastward of the Jordan **River** after all. 2 Chronicles 9:26 says David saw this boundary down in **Egypt** in his reign.

21 the Amorites, the Canaanites, the Girgashites, and the Jebusites." After observing more than twenty lists there are several good guesses why these were listed and no one is any more authorative than the other. It seems this is just a general way of stating all the extents of the land. Obviously because this is **Canaan** we are describing these are probably all people of Ham (then **Canaan**).

Chapter 16

16:1-2

2 So Sarai said to Abram, "See now, the LORD has restrained me from bearing children. Please, go in to my maid; This wasn't foreign to **Abram** or **Sarai.** Their dad had more than one woman in his life (chapter 11)….unless, of course, all but one of his wives was dead. In a sense, even a **maid** was a wife in a sense [as was the "concubine" of Abraham (Genesis 25:1 compared with 1 Chronicles 1:32) as were the hand**maid**s of Leah and Rachel (Genesis 30:1-9)].

perhaps I shall obtain children by her." And Abram heeded the voice of Sarai. If this were God's idea, this was completely acceptable in that culture. This was still a sin if a sin is "falling short of God's glory" (Romans 3:23). Abram presumably knew God's design from his forefathers (Genesis 2). This is only 5th hand information to Abram. Abram did, though, capitulate to his wife…just like Adam.

To be fair, **Abram** did have to sever the animals and keep the birds off of them in the unilateral covenant of chapter 15…so maybe he felt like this was a worthy step to "help God" as well?

16:5

Then Sarai said to Abram, "My wrong *be* upon you! I gave my maid into your embrace; Perhaps she thought she was doing Abram a favor to give him a son. It wasn't working out well with **Sarai.**

16:6-8

So Abram said to Sarai, "Indeed your maid *is* in your hand; do to her as you please." Probably, **Sarai** was hoping **Abram** would somehow take action against the mother of his own son.

7 Now the Some people take this to mean there is only one when in the context we could say "Let's take the car" to our kids when we would never be thought to be saying "there is only one car in the whole world." Rather, it seems best to see that this is **the Angel of the LORD** particular to this episode.

This is not Jesus all the time. Matthew 1 would find Jesus both in the womb of Mary and announcing His own birth to Joseph…at the same time. There are times when **the Angel of the LORD** is contextually a pre-incarnate appearance of Christ, but we need not always assume that it is so (Psalm 34:7, for example).

Verse 13 does seem to say that Hagar believes this is the **LORD,** and it could be that she is correct. She may have been simply making reference to His involvement through this **Angel.**

16:9-12

The Angel of the LORD said to her, "Return to your mistress, If she does not do this then she will most certainly return to Egypt from whence she came (since she was already headed south), and then her decedents would not have been able to get Joseph there (37:28). Furthermore…this is amazing to conceive…Judah would have died in famine (50:20) and we would have had no Savior (humanly speaking Jesus must have come the way that He came), and we would all die in our sins and go to Hell.

and submit yourself under her hand." The Messenger **of the LORD** was sending her back to an austere situation. There is a lesson here for the believer. Some wonder why the New Testament doesn't seek to abolish slavery, but the reader should consider primarily why the Gospel cannot empower a slave? It can!

11 And the Angel of the LORD said to her: "Behold, you *are* **with child, And you shall bear a son.** An Egyptian girl gets the first birth announcement from Heaven in the whole Bible! Jesus and John the Baptist, neither one, were the first [or Samson (Judges 13)]. It is also the first time a **child** is named before his/her birth.

You shall call his name ⁴Ishmael, This means "God hears." We will soon find out that He sees as well.

12 He shall be a wild the other times it is used it is translated "donkey" (**wild** ass of a **man**);

And he shall dwell in the presence of all his brethren." We will find out that Ishmael will have 12 sons.

16:13

Then she called the name of the LORD who spoke to her, You-Are-⁵the-God-Who-Sees; Hagar believes she has been communicating with the **LORD,** then. Exodus 6:1-3 tells us that at this time they did not know God's Name at this time. This is why people named Him after what He did. This is why it is ridiculous to say things like "we worship Him for Who He is; not what He does." We know nothing of Him besides a revelation of His mighty acts.

---

⁴ Lit. *God Hears*
⁵ Heb. *El Roi*

Genesis 17

17:1

When Abram was ninety-nine years old, 13 years elapse between chapters, then. **the LORD appeared to Abram and said to him,** God first appeared to him 24 years ago (12:4). This is significant. It has been 24 years since He received a promise—the main thing, of which, is a natural-born descendant. The lesson is that "hearing from God" does not mean immediate movement by God. We'll see more of this with Joseph.[85]

"I am Almighty God; Now, the first person we're told that knows that *Elohim* is *Jehovah* is Eve. She used both names when she said "I have gotten a man" (chapter 4). In Genesis 14, Melchizedek gives God the name *El Elyon.* Later in chapter 16 we have an Egyptian girl calling Him *El Roi.* They are calling *Jehovah* certain things that they give Him names to reflect His actions. Of course, these names/actions reflect His character: He "is" certain things so He "does" certain things. In other words, it is impossible but that He "does." God "does." Psalm 150 says "Praise Him for His Mighty acts." It is impossible to know Him without knowing His Works. His character drives His Works which drives our worship.[86]

Take *Elohim* in Genesis 1:1: The first thing we know about God is not a characteristic outside of work, but rather a work that tells of His characteristics and attributes. The God of Heaven is not merely propositional or faith-based dogma. He works. John 5:17 is the testimony of Jesus that "My Father works until now…"

---

[85] 17 when he dreams; 39 when he sees fulfillment.

[86] In post resurrection Christology, we have a Jesus Whose wounds are in His hands. Even in Revelation 5, we have a "Lamb as it has been slaughtered" standing in the midst of the elders before the throne. Why do they bow to Him? Revelation 5:9 says it is because "He has redeemed us by His blood out of every kindred, people, tribe, and nation." It is a Christian reality to worship God for what He has done through Christ.

We are approximately 2000 years into human history when we hear of another name for God. Why? Does God take this long? Maybe the answer is in the preceding verse: It has been 13 years since Ishmael was born. Perhaps, Abram needed to hear "This is not hard." We'll soon find out that a 90 year old woman is going to be pregnant. It would be a God Who is **Almighty** to do these things that don't occur every day.

By the way, two other people have changes of names in this chapter: Abram (17:5) & Sarai (17:15). As seen in 16:11, we see that there really are stories in a name.

walk before Me as Enoch did [and did not die (5:21)]. **and be blameless.** As did Noah (6:8-9), and Abraham must do it thematically, with God's grace found there. The implication is that **Abram** has not been so **walk**ing.

2 And I will make My covenant used 10 times in this chapter.

17:3

Then Abram fell on his face, When you see verse 17, we realize that this happened regularly.

a father of many nations. Galatians 3:8 tells us that this along with Genesis 12:1-4 are intended to preach what Paul called the Gospel (Galatians 1:8-9; 3:8).

17:11

and you shall be circumcised in the flesh of your foreskins, and it shall be a sign of the covenant We have **sign**s of the New **covenant** in baptism and the Lord's Supper and we are reminded that the strength of the **covenant** is not the strength of it.

17:15

Then God said to Abraham, "As for Sarai means "contentious"
or "struggled" **your wife, you shall not call her name Sarai, but
Sarah[87] shall be her name.** Fitting, since she'll be the mother of
many nations. God is, again, making a memorial of His Own
Work. Abraham builds altars, and God presents new names (see
17:1 notes). So the story was told of the major change every time
the name was used.

17:17-20

**Then Abraham fell on his face and laughed, and said in his
heart, "Shall a child be born to a man who is one hundred
years old? And shall Sarah, who is ninety years old, bear a
child?"** It is interesting that Paul carefully selects the Genesis 15
account to tell us of Abraham's unwavering faith. Romans 4 says
Abraham was "not weak in faith." If we are not careful to notice
the linkage between Genesis 15:6 and Romans 4:22, we might
think this man's laughter was simply a nervous **laugh** and a happy
laugh. Unfortunately it was doubt. Even Ambrose is quoted as
saying "the fact that Abraham laughed when he had been promised
a son through her was an expression not of unbelief, but of joy...,
[and was effectively saying] as the author of nature you will
effectively stretch its limits"[88] I wish it were so, but the problem is
that we have Abraham's request and God's answer in verse 19.
(Oh that Ishmael might live before you...then God said "no.")
This is really something. Abram really didn't think Sarah was to be
a part of the plan. Certainly if she wasn't when he was 86 and she
was 77 (in chapter 16 when they concocted the plan), how much
less now that he is 99 and she is 90?!

No in all fairness to Abraham, if Romans 4 tells us
anything, it tells us he felt like it could happen when he was 76,

---

[87]*Princess*
[88]Thomas C. Oden, ed. *Ancient Christian Commentary on Scripture,
Old Testament volume II* (Downers Grove, Ill: Intervarsity Press, 2002), 58.

and Sarai was 67 (jelling it with his age of 75 in 12:4 and the likelihood that only a year or so had passed until 15:1-6). Another 10 years seemed difficult; hence, Hagar. Another 13 years above that?! **Laugh**able.

18 And Abraham said to God, "Oh, that Ishmael might live before You!" He loves his son while knowing Ishmael was not the perfect will of God in "blessing the nations" (Galatians 3:8), and yet he wanted him to have this same God's blessed presence in his life. Do you think God heard his prayer? Genesis 25 sure seems to say so! This Ishmael will **beget twelve princes** (verse 20).

Genesis 18

18:1-3

Then the Lord appeared to him by the terebinth trees of Mamre, 13:18 has Abraham living here since he was in his late 70's. Here we are more than 20 years later. 14:13 has one of Abraham's neighbors from here showing up to let Abraham know of some trouble taking place in Lot's life. 15:16, with 14:13, speaking of this place as the habitation of the Amorites, speaks of a day when the Amorites will be wiped out of the entirety of this same land. This is, furthermore (chapter 13), where Abraham built an altar and the LORD met with him there.[89] It was a special place, then, and it became habit to be around where God had first met him.

2 So he lifted his eyes and looked, and behold, three men verse 22 seems to say one of these **men** was the LORD of verse 1. Furthermore, 19:1 identifies the two **men** who were not the LORD as "angels." So, Jehovah and two angels were called **men.**

3 and said, "My Lord, if I have now found favor in Your sight, do not pass on by Your servant. One gets the idea here that Abraham is moving a tad too urgently to assume these were just human passersby. For one thing, how did they get through the, no doubt, surrounding camp?

18:9-12

Then they said to him, "Where *is* Sarah your wife?" So he said, "Here, in the tent." 10 And He said, Here is probably where Abraham became aware that he was talking to God. The "they" of verse 9 became **He** alone in verse 9. Some versions put "the LORD" instead of **He,** but the problem is that this is not a

---

[89]Genesis 4 and Hebrews 11:4 seem to say the testimony that "God met with someone" was the fire He sent to devour their sacrifice.

translation. One will not find "the LORD" in the original text. **"I will certainly return to you according to the time of life,** Some have said this is an Hebraic expression for "next spring."

11 Now Abraham and Sarah were old, well advanced in age; *and* Sarah had passed the age of childbearing. Hebrew euphemism for "past menopause".

12 Therefore Sarah laughed within herself, in 17:17, Abraham laughed. This was either directly given to Moses by the Holy Spirit or Sarah later relayed this to somebody. **saying, "After I have grown old,** the NET Bible says "worn out." **shall I have pleasure, my lord being old also?"** past the age of sex and resulting child bearing.

18:13-14

14 Is anything too hard for the LORD? The context requires a sort of finish to this sentence in our understanding: "is anything too hard for Jehovah Who promised it?" **At the appointed time I will return to you, according to the time of life, and Sarah shall have a son."** Romans 4:17 and following speaks of God breathing life into both Abraham and into Sarah's womb. We spoke in the previous chapter that this was the case back in Genesis 15, but we have two who are dying bringing life and Paul intimates that it was through faith.

18:16-21

At this point, Jehovah has a conversation about what He is going to do with two who are later identified as "angels." If there is a "let us make" in Genesis 1 and a "let us go down" in Genesis 11, it seems reasonable to say that the "us" in both of those situations is "angels" at least.

Then, there is a very strange reality that God appears to be both constraining Himself to space and expressing omnipresence in the very same sentence. He actually appears to have needed to come and visit to know the truth of the matter. On the other hand, He states He will do the visitation yet there is no evidence that this 3rd "man" (Jehovah) actually visits in the same manner in which the angels do. In the next chapter, it is this same "LORD" that rains down from Heaven (19:24).

18:22-23

23 And Abraham came near[90] and said, Here we get into a very strange exchange where Abraham actually believes that Jehovah is going to **destroy.** So whether it was through words here unrecorded, or whether it was through inference from what is recorded, we do not know. One this is certain, **Abraham** is praying like he has not prayed before. He is praying, at least from the reader's perspective, far more for those affected by destruction than he has ever prayed in relation to life—life that would be given to him and would inherit the promises of God. **"Would You also destroy the righteous with the wicked?** It's interesting that he thinks a man that is unwise to choose selfishly and posture himself carelessly is just (Genesis 13-14). When we peek into the next chapter it becomes further intriguing that he thinks one who is so ungodly that his sons in law mock him when he seeks to be serious, and one who is so vulnerable that he can either become easily drunk (resulting in incest) or allowed his children to be educated in such a manner where they can ferment wine, or at least get a man drunk, or at least be mistaken about geography and "who is left upon the earth" (Genesis 19)…is **just!**

18:25-32

---

[90]One must almost assume that Moses, the author, knew of this story in his own intercessory dealings with the LORD [Exodus 32:11 and following (for more see http://www.sermonaudio.com/sermoninfo.asp?SID=51131942363); Numbers 14:13 and following (for more listen to http://www.sermonaudio.com/sermoninfo.asp?SID=75121659137)].

Far be it from You to do such a thing as this, to slay the righteous with the wicked, so that the righteous should be as the wicked; far be it from You! Shall not the Judge of all the earth do right?" The second most wonderful question this chapter (18:14).

27 Then Abraham answered and said, "Indeed now, I who am but dust Interesting reference to his known Adamic lineage. **and ashes have taken it upon myself to speak to the Lord:**

32 Then he said, "Let not the Lord be angry, and I will speak but once more: Suppose ten should be found there?"And He said, "I will not destroy it for the sake of ten." We know he has a wife, two virgin daughters and at least two "sons in law" from the next chapter. That gives us 8. So if **ten** is a number Abraham has in mind, perhaps he was counting servants in his house or a 3rd daughter married to 3rd son in law.

In any case, the reader is seemingly left with two possible realities: either "there was not 10 righteous and so God destroyed the city" or "there was exactly 10 righteous and the LORD needed them removed before He destroyed the city." But what do we make of the fact that there are possibly **ten righteous** counted among the city and only 3 make it out?

Perhaps the real two choices are: "there were not 10 righteous and God destroyed the city" or "there were 10 righteous but only because of those with whom they were associated and the LORD needed them removed before He destroyed the city." **33 So the LORD went His way** presumably to Heaven (19:24)? **as soon as He had finished speaking with Abraham; and Abraham returned to his place** his tent, perhaps (19:27-28)?

Chapter 19

19:1-2

Now the two angels from the previous chapter, "two men" who left Abraham and the 3rd man (18:16). If Jesus had gone instead, they would have repented (Matthew 11:23).

came to Sodom in the evening, Is this the same day that begun in 18:1? **and Lot was sitting in the gate** As seen in Ruth 4, this is where leaders of a city might have been set to make decisions. This should tell us Lot is relatively shrewd to become a leader in **Sodom.** The reader will remember that he has been here, really, since chapter 13. Interesting parallel with the opening verses of the previous chapter—perhaps drawing a contrast (although both Abraham and **Lot** showed hospitality).

19:3

But he insisted strongly; Either the custom of hospitality or Lot's knowledge of the kind of people found in his city drove him to constrain them.

19:4-5[91]

Now before they lay down, the men of the city, the men of Sodom, both old and young, Sodomites teach their children to be Sodomites.

5 And they called to Lot and said to him, "Where are the men who came to you tonight? [i]**Bring them out to us that we** [j]**may know them** *carnally***."** The very character that was causing them to destroy Sodom is being revealed on the night they visit.

---

[91]See under 38:12-16 as well.
[i]Judg. 19:22
[j]Rom. 1:24, 27; Jude 7

19:6-8

8 See now, I have two daughters who have not known a man;
Either these are merely betrothed to the sons in law found later in
the passage or Lot has more than these **two daughters.**

**please, let me bring them out to you, and you may do to them
as you wish;** And somehow, Peter is driven to believe that Lot is a
just and righteous man (2 Peter 2:7-8) just as Jesus put Lot and
Noah near each other in the Olivet Discourse so Peter does in his
2nd chapter.

only do nothing to these men, Again, maybe it was the gravity of
hospitality, or it was a fear of what the men would do to the guests,
or…maybe Lot knew what the two angels were there to do and that
they would not hopefully allow the two daughters to be misused.
It's hard to know how sinister Lot is within this scenario.

19:9-11

**11 And they struck the men who *were* at the doorway of the
house with blindness, both small and great, so that they
became weary *trying* to find the door.** This is desperate
sinfulness. Romans 1:28-33 seems to describe this.

19:14

**So Lot went out and spoke to his sons-in-law, who had married
his daughters, and said, "Get up, get out of this place; for the
LORD will destroy this city!"** There is relatively little favorably
said about **city** life in Scripture.

But to his sons-in-law he seemed to be joking. It seems that they
also live in his house (or they went out a back entrance?). This is
the same Lot who had apparently failed in teaching his children.

They do, after all, seem to know how to get dad out of his mind (see the end of the chapter). Maybe they saw their father-in-law drunk and acting stupid and **joking.**

19:15-17

16 And while he lingered, the men took hold of his hand, his wife's hand, and the hands of his two daughters, the LORD being merciful to him, yet Lot lost his house. See God's **mercy** brings loss as well.

17 So it came to pass, when they had brought them outside, that he said, "Escape for your life! Do not look behind you nor stay anywhere in the plain. Escape to the mountains, lest you be destroyed." Same word found in the previous chapter when Abraham bargains with God.

19:18-20

Then Lot said to them, "Please, no, my lords! Here is another disagreement with God—which seems strangely reminiscent of Satan toward Eve in chapter 3.

20 See now, this city *is* near *enough* to flee to, and it *is* a little one; Even though God wouldn't spare Sodom for 9 or less, somehow He wouldn't see the need to destroy a **little** city? **please let me escape there (*is* it not a little one?) and my soul shall live."** See the difference between the bargaining of Abraham in chapter 18, brought by unselfish intercession, and this bargaining hatched out of a lust for comfort. Then, we see the difference between Lot and Abimelech in the next chapter who knew that God could destroy a small nation for the sin of a few and he wished to obtain mercy. The character of this godless man Abimelech is more in keeping with Abraham than Lot.

19:23-25

24 Then the LORD rained brimstone and fire on Sodom and Gomorrah, from the LORD out of the heavens. It could be involving the pits into which the kings fell in chapter 14.

26 But his wife looked back behind him, and she became a pillar of salt. Just as the brimstone and fire appeared to fall from the heavens, so she may have merely appeared to become **a pillar of salt.** She loved Sodom. Her husband was important in that city, and that made her feel important. Not only did he appear to be a jokester to his sons in law, but he was not preparing his wife for the severe actions of God either. Luke 17:32 uses this little episode as a teaching tool concerning readiness for the coming of Jesus.

19:27-29

And Abraham went early in the morning to the place where he had stood before the LORD. 18:22 begins this entire episode with the Lord and Abraham standing together. The reader should need to see what a chiasm is: a story ends where it began.

29 And it came to pass, when God destroyed the cities of the plain, that God remembered Abraham, This reminds the reader of Noah (8:1). These themes are more repetitive than one thinks as we have now seen Eve/Satan, Noah's remembrance, Abraham's bargaining, and Abimelech's bargaining all in this episode, but then we find some echoes of Noah with Ham in the following episode.

19:30-33[92]

Then Lot went up out of Zoar Wow! He found the energy somehow!

---

[92]See 38:1-5 as well.

31 Now the firstborn said to the younger, "Our father *is* old, and *there is* no man on the earth to come in to us Just as the survivors of Noah's flood were sure they were alone on the earth which may have led them to a despondent drunkenness. This isn't a hard comparison: God destroys the many and saves a few—even if it is a local issue here. Don't forget about "rain" in both stories either (19:24).

32 Come, let us make our father drink wine, It should seem odd that the first two times **wine** is mentioned in the Bible it leads to shame.

33 So they made their father drink wine that night. And the firstborn went in and lay with her father, and he did not know when she lay down or when she arose. Where did they get this deviant knowledge? Where did they learn to justify their choices? Sodom. Let us not forget the reason we are analyzing their choices to begin with is because their father had already made bad choices (as far back as "pitching his tent toward Sodom" in Genesis 13).

19:38

And the younger, she also bore a son and called his name Ben-Ammi; he *is* the father of the people of Ammon to this day. Two godless and troublesome people are then decedents from Lot. One of our most precious prophecies of Jesus (Numbers 24) and one of the most beautiful stories of love in the Bible (Ruth 1-4) come from the Moabites.

Genesis 20

20:1

And Abraham journeyed from there to the South, in some versions it says "Negev." **and dwelt between Kadesh** The place where Numbers 11-14 will show us a potentially 11-day journey taking 38 years (says Deuteronomy) **and Shur,** These places of Hagar's meeting with the angel in chapter 16.

20:2

Now Abraham said of Sarah his wife, "She is my sister." Here we go again, only this time she is not 66 as in chapter 12; she is 91. Whoa! She must have been amazingly pretty!

Another thing to consider is that we have roughly 1800-1900 years between Genesis 1 and Genesis 11. Now, since Genesis 12, we've passed only 24-25 years.[93]

And Abimelech Means "my father is king," and is merely a title such as "Pharaoh" or "Candice" (Acts 8). **king** remember, we have ten different "kings" mentioned in chapter 14 so there's no need to see every **king** as a larger "king" in today's sense. **of Gerar sent and took Sarah.** Just as Pharaoh did. Perhaps this was a diplomatic move to have peace with a fellow king? To marry his sister?[94] Marrying into other royal families appears to be a pretty common practice even in Solomon's day.

20:3

But ᶠGod came to Abimelech ᵍin a dream by night, and said to him, "Indeed you are a dead man because of the woman whom

---

[93]Genesis 17-Genesis 20 is a mere year.
[94]Proposed to me by SRBC deacon Walter Creighton.
ᶠPs. 105:14
ᵍJob 33:15

you have taken, for she is a man's wife." Notice that the charge is understandable to this **Abimelech**, and he even defends himself regarding the charge. Please do take note, then, that there is a universal appreciation and understanding of certain ethical/legal expectations across cultural and geographical lines. Obviously, though, Abraham didn't have a whole lot of faith that that sense of right and wrong would have curtailed their lustful theft of his wife—twice now.

20:4-5

But Abimelech had not come near her; and he said, "Lord, will You slay a righteous Here again, we are amazed that this ruler thinks his folks are **righteous** just as Abraham supposed Lot and his clan were **righteous** (18:23).

nation also? How long ago did Sodom get destroyed? Perhaps months since the last few chapters took a year. Somebody has been a testimony to Abimelech. He knows somebody has spared a nation by appealing to supposed righteousness. **5 Did he not say to me, 'She is my sister'? And she, even she herself said, 'He is my brother.' In the integrity of my heart** We see two very surprising things: Abimelech thinks his folks are "righteous" (verse 4), and he says that his heart has **integrity**! Now, of course, we could work around this and say "He is only saying he has **integrity** regarding this situation," but even so…he is using some pretty spiritual language, is he not?[95]

20:6

And God said to him in a dream, "Yes, I know that you did this in the integrity of your heart. For I also withheld you from sinning against Me; Yes, God was the one who taught Joseph that

---

[95]This is a very good similarity to the words of Job's wife in Job's 2nd chapter. Perhaps this is a good proof showing the Mosaic authorship (at least, in part) of Job.

to sin against a man was to really sin against God (Genesis 39:9). In both cases, it was the sin of taking another man's wife. **therefore I did not let you touch her.** It's been less than a year since the birth announcement of Isaac. This is a real problem! If God doesn't intervene, Abimelech could be given credit for the conception of Isaac!

20:7-9

Now therefore, restore the man's wife; for he is a prophet, and he will pray This is the first time this term is used in the Bible and it is a man asking for something on behalf of somebody else. Furthermore, the first function of a prophet was praying for somebody else (intercession) **for you and you shall live. But if you do not restore her, know that you shall surely die,** So we see that impending death is the same as being "a dead man" (verse 3). Furthermore, since this is the next instance of somebody being called "dead" or seen as "dying" after Genesis 2, there is no point in seeing the Edenic account as a sort of "spiritual death" as touted by so many preachers and teachers, and rather see Adam and Eve as "good as dead" (as Abimelech is here) if they eat of the forbidden fruit. **you and all who are yours."** Numbers 16 (Korah's household) and Joshua 6 (Achan's household) show this principle being carried out in the rest of this saga.

9 And Abimelech called Abraham and said to him, "What have you done to us? How have I offended you, that you have brought on me and on my kingdom a great sin? Again, when the leader of a kingdom is in deep sin, it appears that the kingdom itself is being counted sinful. **You have done deeds to me that ought not to be done."** For somebody who does not appear to know *Elohim* or *El Elyon*, this is a pretty refined sense of right and wrong.

20:11-15

And Abraham said, "Because I thought, surely the fear of God is not in this place; Abraham, on the other hand, has a very low view of this nation's sense of morality. "I was pretty sure you folks steal wives and murder people."

12 But indeed she is truly my sister. She is the daughter of my father, but not the daughter of my mother; and she became my wife. An explanation that would have been helpful in chapter 12. **13 And it came to pass, when God caused me to wander from my father's house,** flashback to 12:1-3.

14 Then Abimelech took sheep, oxen, and male and female servants, and gave them to Abraham; and he restored Sarah his wife to him. Abraham gets richer again because of God just as he did in the Genesis 12 episode. **15 And Abimelech said, "See, my land is before you; dwell where it pleases you."** It is all his anyway (Genesis 15). This is, furthermore, like Satan offering Jesus the "nations of the world" (Matthew 4) only to realize they are all His anyway (Matthew 28:18).

On the other hand, this is God's way of allowing Abraham to reap what he sowed in Genesis 13 where he gave Lot this very same offer.

20:16

Then to Sarah he said, "Behold, I have given your brother a thousand pieces of silver; indeed this vindicates you before all who are with you and before everybody." Thus she was rebuked. This word has some other intricacies which may provide a positive rather than negative translation. In other words, her record was purged. She was not known as she who was intimate with this man and she was allowed to leave.

20:17-18

So Abraham prayed to God; and God healed Abimelech, his wife, and his female servants. Here's a wonderful token of God's sovereignty: **Abimelech** is experiencing God and learning more about Jehovah-God, but it was done as a result of Abraham's strange and perhaps sinful dealings.

Chapter 21

21:14[96]

21:27

So Abraham took sheep and oxen and gave them to Abimelech, and the two of them made can also be translated "cut" which makes a lot of sense given what we know what occurred in Genesis 15 when the unilateral **covenant** was made by God toward **Abraham.** These are different than the "seven ewe lambs" in verse 30 which served as witnesses among **Abimelech**'s flock.

21:31

Therefore he called that place Beersheba, because the two of them swore an oath there. The exchange of animals (witnesses) and the naming of a well (meaning "well of the seven", named proleptically by Moses a little earlier in the book, 21:14) serve as a marking of this covenant.

21:33

---

[96]See under 28:18-22.
[97]Pictured to the right and provided by my logos software ("Images from a Standard Bible Dictionary").

Then *Abraham* planted a tamarisk tree[97] **in Beersheba,** Seeing that in the next few verses of the next chapter they end up in Mariah, they make good distance in three days. **and there called on the name of the Lord, the Everlasting God.** Again, not knowing His personal Name (Exodus 6:1-3), they name **God** things that reflect His character and actions. Genesis 3:22 is the first time this word for **everlasting** is used and it is **God** keeping man from living forever in a fallen state. Genesis 6:3 shows **God** unwilling to **everlasting**ly fight with man—it is not good for man or glorifying to **God.** Genesis 9:12 (with 9:16) & 13:15 describe that **God** makes **everlasting** covenants. For the first time, then, **God** is not using the word. **Abraham** is using the word, and He is using it to remind **God** of a day when there will be no striving for the land **God** had given to him. This promise with this man will do until **God** serves His **everlasting**

covenant. "My dad owns the entire block, but I promise I won't step on your grass (for now)" is the equivalent to this covenant with another man. A timeless **God** can make timeless covenants and we can continue to believe and walk on in peace.

"This attention on Abraham's deity as the Eternal One"[98] unlike the moody and temporary relationships of lesser deities found

---

[98]K. A. Mathews, *Genesis 11:27–50:26*, vol. 1B, The New American

within the created order, particularly the Canaanites. What could Abraham do here? He is needing to "live peaceably" (Romans 12:18) with someone who, for all intensive purposes, has no claim on any of the land—not even the land on his side of the boundary. God had given it to Abraham (Genesis 13:15)! This is maddening and disappointing in the present and the way Abraham deals with this difficulty is to appeal to a timeless God Who makes timeless promises. More difficult than this is that the Hebrews writer admits that Abraham did not receive these promises (Hebrews 11:13), but only in the eyes of faith—knowing that a timeless God would make good on His timeless promises in a world to come! This is nearly unclear until you see that this is precisely what Abraham was expecting in the next chapter when the very person who is to be receiving these promises is likely to be killed before he can receive them or have children that will receive them! So in a few short verses here (despite the chapter break) Abraham is not only facing the question of when he will receive the land promise (Genesis 13:15), but is also facing the question of how he will receive the promise of many children (13:15)! Consequently, this potentially threatens not only the first order fulfillment of the land promise (to himself) but to an understandably-difficult-to-grasp second order fulfillment of the land promise to his son in answer to Hebrews 11:13.

It is after one difficult grasp and before the other that Abraham appeals to the **Everlasting God.** He **everlasts,** or better said, outlasts our limitations; outlasts our consternations.

Ecclesiastes 3:11 makes us contemplate eternity, to be sure.

Commentary (Nashville: Broadman & Holman Publishers, 2005), 283.

Chapter 22

22:1-2[99]

2 Then He said, "Take now your son, This has already happened to him concerning another **son** (21:12). **^byour only** *son* **Isaac,** is 36 years old in the next chapter when his mother dies, but if there is only 10 years between the chapters then he is 26. Maybe it's 15 years? Well, he's 21 year old here. **whom you love,** and **whom** has no children to receive the promise (21:12).

and go to the land of Moriah, 2 Chronicles 3:1 shows us this is where Solomon builds his temple. They were in Beersheeba in the last chapter. This is 50 miles away and that is direct mileage. There are plenty of mountains.

22:3-5

So Abraham rose early in the morning just as he did in 21:14 after troubling news concerning his other **son.**

5 And Abraham said to his young men, "Stay here with the donkey; the lad can easily be 20 years old since perspective places this against a 125 year old father. Also, we see this regarding Benjamin in Genesis 43, that he was in his 30's and called a **lad.** With his mother dying in Isaac's 37th year in the next chapter, we could say that Isaac is either a toddler [unlikely if he's carrying the wood (22:6)] or 37, but it seems like a medium of 15-20 years old is quite reasonable.

and I will go yonder and worship, In **Abraham**'s mind, this was going to be Isaac. It was not free to worship to Abraham (or David, according to the last chapter of 2 Samuel) **and we will come back to you."** Hebrews 11:17-19 shows us that Abraham believed God could raise His Son back up if he had to offer him for this "burnt

---

[99]See also under 28:18-22.

offering." He would have been ashes on the rocks, yet it seems **Abraham** expected him to be raised if it had come to that.

22:6-7

So Abraham took the wood of the burnt offering and laid *it* on Isaac just as he did upon Hagar (21:14). **his son;** John 19:17 shows us this was Christ carrying His cross in the telescopic view.

22:8

And Abraham said, "My son, God will provide for Himself the ʰlamb for a burnt offering." Another pre-law (Exodus 12:3-6), Mosaic reality (in addition to the clean/unclean animals distinction of Genesis 6 and the levirate marriage of Genesis 39:5-6). **So the two of them went together.** In the Calvary perspective (Luke 24:27; 24:44), God was with His Son all the way to the cross (Isaiah 53:10). Sweet communion all the way to the noon hour on the day of death.

22:9-10

Then they came to the place in the Christ picture, this is **God**'s good planning choosing the place and the means by which His Son would die (1 Peter 1:20). **of which God had told him. And Abraham built an altar there and placed the wood in order; and he bound Isaac his son** Ishmael was also set aside for death (21:15).

and laid him on the altar, upon the wood. There is no indication that he fought his father. He had been watching his father live by faith for his entire life—hearing stories of Abraham's departure from the comforts of the hometown in his 70's. Incidentally, this is the first time God tells Abraham to do something without his responding with questions. **10 And Abraham stretched out his hand and took the knife to slay his son.** In the Jesus/Father

101

perspective, God held the hammer. Isaiah 53:10-11 shows us it was the Father who "bruised [His Son]."

Here is where Isaac no longer pictures Christ and the picture of Christ switches to the "ram."

22:11-12

But the Angel of the LORD called to him from heaven Just as he had done, in 21:17, to Hagar. It seems that, at least in this case (and in 21:17) that this is in fact a theophany—otherwise, I have some real questions: Like how did the **angel** see all of this from that far away…unless **heaven** is closer than we think? Or how did **the angel** speak from that far away…unless **heaven** is closer than we think? If this is God (another question), how did he not "know" already what Abraham would do (verse 12)? If He did not know, then, what does this say about absolute knowledge? This doesn't even qualify as "middle knowledge" because "middle knowledge" means He knows all possible outcomes. So, I guess because of this, I am going to say that the **angel of the LORD** is not God and for some reason God allowed His **angel** to discover something for some reason.

12 And He said, "Do not lay your hand on the lad, or do anything to him; for ᵐnow I know that you fear God, since you have not withheld your son, your only *son,* Isaac is in his 30's probably so this is strange terminology, isn't it? **from Me."**

22:13-14

Then Abraham lifted his eyes just as Hagar was able to all of the sudden see God's provision (21:19).

and looked, and there behind *him was* **a ram caught in a thicket by its horns.** And only by **its horns,** or it may not have been without blemish. Christ was so pictured (1 Peter 1:18-19). **So**

102

Abraham went and took the ram, a male sheep that can still breed.

14 And Abraham called the name of the place, [3]The-LORD-Will-Provide; as it is said *to* this day, "In the Mount of the LORD it shall be provided." What would be provided in the **Mount?** The Lamb (22:7). Where is **the Mount of the LORD?** In Exodus it is Sinai, so since they are rather at Moriah, it seems that **Mount of the LORD** is anywhere God establishes His covenant. Since Jesus is the mediator of the New Covenant and gives His life close by Moriah, we can only assume that this is a prophecy of John 1:29. Surely Isaiah 2:3 shows us that Zion would be **the Mount of the LORD** is in Jerusalem, and this prophecy should remove all doubt. In Genesis 14:18, we are told that Melchizedek is king in the very place where this story takes place. Was he there in that place?

22:15-19

Then the Angel of the LORD called to Abraham a second time out of heaven, Sometimes it is God (Exodus 3:1-3), but other times this is not so.

17 blessing I will [p]bless you, and multiplying I will multiply your descendants as the stars of the heaven and as the sand which *is* on the seashore; and your descendants shall possess the gate of their enemies. Much the same promise he received in 21:12.

19 So Abraham returned to his young men, just like he said he would. **and they rose and went together to [v]Beersheba; and Abraham dwelt at Beersheba.** Still, as last chapter. The story then ends where it began.

---

[h]Gen. 4:26; 12:8; 13:4; 26:25
[b]Gen. 22:12, 16; John 3:16; Heb. 11:17; 1 John 4:9
[h]John 1:29, 36

Chapter 23

23:1-2

Sarah lived one hundred and twenty-seven years; Which means Isaac is now 36 years old. This means, according to chapter 25, that Sarah never met his wife. ***these were* the years of the life of Sarah. 2 So Sarah died in Kirjath Arba (that *is*, Hebron)** which means that **Abraham** travelled 40 miles from Beersheeba (22:19) at some point in those more than 3 decades covering only Genesis 22 in the Biblical record.

in the land of Canaan, and Abraham came to mourn First time in the Bible someone's death is being **mourn**ed.

23:3-4

Then Abraham stood up from before his dead, and spoke to the sons of Heth, the Hittites: they came from Ham (says Genesis 10). Most of the folks in this neck of the woods known as "Canaan" came from Canaan, son of Ham. **saying, 4 "I *am* a foreigner and a visitor among you. Give me property for a burial place** This is also the first time in the Bible someone is **buri**ed.

23:5-6

6 "Hear us, my lord: You *are* a mighty prince their first acquaintance with him was over 60 years ago and he had an army of over 300 then. **among us; bury your dead in the choicest of our burial places.** Abraham was a major mover with his small town worth of population traveling together, and his existence among them was a boost to their economy. **None of us will withhold from you his burial place, that you may bury your dead."** We should consider that he did not cremate her. See my commentary on Mark (a footnote in chapter 15 surrounding the **buri**al of Jesus). If we are right in seeing the story of Job as occurring in these times (see my appendix on authorship in my commentary on Job) then they may have had similar beliefs on the resurrection (Job 19:25) and **burial** best shows faith in the resurrection.

23:17

So the field of Ephron which *was* in Machpelah, which *was* before Mamre, We see from 13:10 & 18:1 that Abraham has been in and around this piece of land for a great many years (decades by this time).

Seems like a good time for a discussion on "Christians & Cremation":

There are, perhaps, other debates to have...like whether a family should have a funeral or memorial service for their loved one; or whether the church and its leadership should have something to say in these family processes; or, whether a church should have its own cemetery to the exclusion of unbelievers...but those debates will have to wait for another time.

We do have families that have been faced with deaths and they are concerned about budgeting and they are concerned about debt and you can save 60% of costs by having a loved one cremated. We don't think it's because they love their loved one any less. We don't think it's because they don't want their loved one to be cared for or honored. In some cases, most of the time, it is nothing but expedient either financially or even to the point where many people are not even having funeral services because it's emotionally expedient. Here are some reasons that I feel like you should not choose cremation for your loved one:

1. It seems that there is an honorable way to care for that which God gave to be the temple of His spirit while on earth. 1 Corinthians 6:15-20 indicates that the reason we behave

ourselves while living is because we are the house of God. Perhaps it is a stretch, but **it seems there are better ways to dispose of that which was the house of God than burning.** There is a biblical stewardship of this body, it seems. Why not make stewardship decisions now that your children or others behind you would otherwise have to make? Moreover, this is a decision that the community of faith should be able to approve. If weddings should be that which the church observes, how much more the funeral? How much more the burial of the loved one?

This is a major opportunity to show respect for the contribution this person made in your life. It is hard to imagine burning someone's remains as being this "show of respect."

2. Burning, in Leviticus, was a demonstration of God's consuming wrath poured out on the specific sacrifice, and the finality of God's consuming fire. The priests are to burn these sacrifices up completely. That's what the Roman Catholic Church did with John Wycliffe at the Council of Constance. They exhumed his bones and burned them and through them in the river. He was still haunting them even after his death so they said, "Dig up his bones and burn them." That was a way of communicating finality. "We're done with him. He will never bother us again." Burial, however, does not speak of finality. **Burial is a witness to an enduring reality**—such as in Ecclesiastes 3:14. Burial grounds become resurrection grounds.

3. John 19:40 speaks to the fact that **it was the custom of the Jews to bury.** Paul said, "To the Jews was committed the oracles of God," (Romans 9:1-4) so certainly the method by which the Jews took care of bodies should be an example to Christians if the oracles of God were committed to them. They become for us very foundational and we need a legitimate reason for abandoning a Jewish custom.[100] Lazarus was buried, at great expense, as seen in John 11.

---

mJames 2:21, 22

How many guys did it take to carry Joseph from Egypt in a box? How many times did they think, "this is getting a little old. He's not going to know. Let's just burying him right here?" There is no way Joseph wanted to wake up in Egypt. He wanted to be in the Promised Land. Since we are recipients of the relationship of the Covenanting God, perhaps we should adopt some of those old practices if they reflect the God of the Covenant until, like Peter regarding their diet, we receive further revelation.

4. **Burning is usually a treatment God uses for His enemies.** It is as if He is forecasting their future after death. We get an account of Moses being buried. However, God burnt Korah.[101] He burned up the sons of Aaron, Nadab and Abihu.[102]

5. **We are most like Christ in burial, not burning.** Some accounts on the linens and the perfumes and the ointments were almost 50 pounds of weight, a considerable cost. Earlier in Passion Week, Mary anointed Jesus with a very costly perfume and Jesus said that she anointed His body for burial. They loved him Jesus. "Yes, he's gone but we can still manifest our love for Jesus."

6. **We have a place to respect the departed.** While we understand one can still go to a mausoleum to see a collection of ashes in an urn, this more speaks to the idea of an outright "cremation and sprinkling the ashes somewhere" sort of scenario. Being able to visit and rethink God's work in the life of a loved one is a privilege that we feel honored in which to partake in view of our increasingly busy world. It's a place to plant flowers, to clean headstones, to tell stories, to prompt questions, etc.... God's people are consistently required to build monuments for His glory, and we can always go and remember and tell stories at a marker.

7. **It is a traditional, Christian practice to bury one's dead.** It is not that we only have two options: be archaic; or, be

---

[3]Heb. *YHWH Yireh*
[p]Gen. 17:16; 26:3, 24

107

progressive. No, it is possible to enjoy both technological advancements and to preserve some meaningful norms that depict Christian consensus. In other words, sometimes we do things because "we have always done it that way" and our identity as Christians is important. 2 Thessalonians 3 says "We command you, brethren, in the name of our Lord Jesus Christ, that you withdraw yourselves from every brother that walks disorderly, and not after the tradition which he received of us. For yourselves know how you ought to follow us..." We don't want to reduce this to his merely bringing us some sort of extra-canonical body of truth that we're supposed to follow, but certainly there were some things that were not on the level with doctrine but were still important enough to be observed.[103]

If we're going to be Christian, let's be distinctively Christian. "Learn not the way of the heathen" (Jeremiah 10). While some brethren think that means you shouldn't have a Christmas tree in the context, it seems there are some more weighty matters, especially in the church today.

The only time we find Jews/Israelites/Hebrews burning remains is out of disgust for something distinctively heathen. Josiah burned the remains of wicked priests in 2 Chronicles 34:1-4. It's as if the extent of the treatment of these deceased was less important than the actual getting rid of them.

Conclusion: If you have had your loved one cremated, you may be wondering how that affects the resurrection. In Genesis 22nd chapter, Abraham believed that God could resurrect a cremated body or he would not have had the mind of burning his son, a burnt offering, and then promising their companions that they would be back after worship. Knowing that he was about to kill his son if God didn't intervene, he was willing to "offer" his son and yet he made the promise, "We'll be right back." Abraham believed that God could raise up his son from ashes on rock, if necessary, to fulfill his promise through the seed, Isaac. I leave you with this

---

[v]Gen. 21:31

little nugget: get some life insurance.

Chapter 24

24:4

Abraham came from "the other side," and knew the harm of his family if they married outside the faith.

24:10-17

Then the servant probably Eliezer when compared with 15:1-3, and I am not alone in this estimation.[104] **took ten of his master's camels and departed, for all his master's goods were in his hand. And he arose and went to Mesopotamia, to the city of Nahor.** The place of the family of Abraham's brother. Genesis 11:22-23 shows that Abraham's brother is named after their grandfather. **11 And he made his camels kneel down outside the city by a well of water at evening time, the time when women go out to draw water.** A cultural note, here, is given. **12 Then he said, "O LORD God of my master Abraham, please give me success this day,** other versions of the Bible (like the Douay-Rheims) see this as a figure of speech in the original and translate it as "meet me today" **and show kindness to my master Abraham.**

15 And it happened, before he had finished speaking, that behold, Rebekah, who was born to Bethuel, Genesis 11:20-22 is a forecast of this passage as well—showing us the birth of **Bethuel.**

son of Milcah, Who is not only the **the wife of Nahor,** but is also the daughter of Haran, Nahor's brother. So, Milcah, according to Genesis 11 married her uncle which means that she is her own aunt. Furthermore, this story will show that Abraham's son Isaac will marry Abraham's great niece.

---

[104]James Ussher *The Annals of the World* (Green Forest, AR: Master Books, Inc., 2003), para. 94.

16 Now the young woman was very beautiful to behold, a virgin; did the servant know this was a virgin? Probably. There were garments of a harlot and garments of a widow (Genesis 38), so probably—virgins had particular apparel as well.

17 And the servant ran to meet her and said, "Please let me drink a little water from your pitcher." A senior citizen is now running towards a woman he doesn't know. If Abraham was 76 or 77 when he spoke of Eleazer in 15:1-3, and Abraham is now 136 (having had a wife that died at the age of 127), then this Eleazer is about 60 years old—and that's if he was newborn in 15:1-3.

24:18-23

20 Then she quickly emptied her pitcher into the trough, ran so she runs after the servant runs (24:17), and later Laban runs out to him (24:29).

21 And the man, wondering at her, remained silent so as to know whether the LORD had made his journey prosperous or not. What? He's watching it and wondering this? Perhaps he was watching to make sure she was going to complete the errand and see if it is God's doing. He's not waiting for a feeling or a revelation or having multiple conversations. He is standing back and watching about how God performs His will in the circumstances of life. "Is this really happening?"

22 So it was, when the camels had finished drinking, I've read a National Geographic article which says that "a thirsty camel can drink 30 gallons of water in 13 minutes." Let's just say they're half thirsty, then we need 150 gallons of water for these 10 camels. If she has a 5 gallon pitcher, carrying 40 pounds of water, then she takes 40 pounds of water 30 times. What if it was a 2 gallon pitcher? She had to make 75 trips. **that the man took a golden nose ring weighing half a shekel, and two bracelets for her**

111

wrists weighing ten shekels of gold, "Manners and Customs" indicates that a "shekel" is a Hebrew measurement of weight equal to ½ ounce. So 5.5 ounces of gold. It is well above $1200 an ounce today. Therefore, we have $6500 worth of gold being given to this lady. From where did these great riches come? Several times God made Abraham rich (verse 35) through a series of, humanly speaking, poor choices (Egypt, Gerar, etc…)—at least in part. Yes, God is using things that appear "unfortunate" to make future endeavors possible.

24:27-28

And he said, "Blessed be the LORD God of my master Abraham, who has not forsaken His mercy and His truth toward my master. As for me, being on the way, He acknowledges, after all, that the "journey" of verse 21 is indeed prosperous as it is the same Hebrew word here. Verse 42 and 48 speak of this very same "journey" or "way" as well.

24:29-31

Now Rebekah had a brother whose name *was* Laban, is the father dead? No (24:50). Perhaps he was running the family business and household just as Isaac was Abraham's.

31 And he said, "Come in, O blessed of the LORD! So how does Laban know this **LORD?** Their fathers both heard from God (last several verses of chapter 11). To be more specific, Isaac's father and Rebekah's grandfather are brothers (11:29; 24:15; 25:20).

24:32-33

Then the man came to the house. And he unloaded the camels, traveling provisions and the bride price for the future bride of Isaac. This is also wonderfully Christological for those of us who will be coming back to our bridegroom (Galatians 3:7)—especially since God has given all things to His Son (32:35; Hebrews 1:4).

24:34-41

35 The LORD has blessed my master greatly, and he has become great; and He has given him flocks and herds, silver and gold, male and female servants, and camels and donkeys. Eliezer, was born in Abraham's house (15:1-3) if this is the same servant. What a mighty man this servant was to seek the notoriety of his master and his son! If Abraham was 75 or so years old and now Abraham is 140 (25:20), the servant has been with him many years and is himself nearly 8 decades old.

40 But he said to me, 'The LORD, before whom I walk, will send His angel with you and prosper your way; Just as He did in Jericho (Joshua 2:9).

24:45-49

46 And she made haste and let her pitcher down from her *shoulder,* and said, 'Drink, and I will give your camels a drink also.' She seems to have been working alone [perhaps not (24:61)], then—despite her family's riches.

49 Now if you will deal kindly and truly with my master, tell me. And if not, tell me, that I may turn to the right hand or to the left." Laban is now being pressed to make a choice.

24:50-51

Then Laban and Bethuel 24:24, the son of Nahor, the brother of Abraham.

24:52-53

113

And it came to pass, when Abraham's servant heard their words, that he worshiped the LORD, *bowing himself* to the earth. What a servant! He loves God, and desires the will of his master—having been the heir apparent if Isaac is not born (15:2-3). **53 Then the servant brought out jewelry of silver, jewelry of gold, and clothing, and gave *them* to Rebekah. He also gave precious things to her brother and to her mother.** He already gave **Rebekah** stuff at the well valued in the thousands of dollars, and that was a picture of the "earnest of the Spirit" (Ephesians 1:12-13) and here is a picture, now, of the bride getting more of what He intends for her. This happens to benefit those who are not a part of the covenant just as Laban benefits because of Jacob's labor in the chapters to come (as well as Potiphar's house because of Joseph's work).

24:56

And he said to them, "Do not hinder me, Brother and dad say "go" (verse 51), but the mother gets involved and they want ten more days (verse 55), which seemed like a lack of progress to the servant. Maybe they are trying to get a better bride price? Maybe there were more things on the camels?

24:57-58

58 Then they called Rebekah and said to her, "Will you go with this man?" And she said, "I will go." This sounds like a marriage vow. This helps us with what looks like quite an informal ceremony (24:66). This tells us that a steward/servant can do a lot on behalf of his master—to include making covenant contracts. After the Sovereign act of God to put these two in front of each other…she still had a choice. We need to remember that there was no "yes, I'll go" until the servant showed up at her well.

24:59-60

60 And they blessed Rebekah and said to her: "Our sister, *may* you *become The mother of* thousands of ten thousands; And may your descendants possess The gates of those who hate them." Or **"may** they possess the cities of their enemies." This is the same thing the angel promised Abraham in Genesis 19.

24:62-65

Now Isaac came from the way of Beer Lahai Roi, The "well of the God Who Sees" first named after what occurred to Hagar (16:13-14) some 54 years earlier. It was also a place where Isaac's family had dwelt previously (20:1). **for he dwelt in the South.** North of Egypt, but quite **south.** We last see they were near Hebron (23:2). **63 And Isaac went out to meditate** some have said this could also be translated as "mourning," which makes good sense contextually since he needed comfort (24:67). **in the field in the evening;** probably doing normal sheep-tending things.

64 Then Rebekah lifted her eyes, and when she saw Isaac she dismounted It is often translated as "fell" and makes this a comical verse as she "fell **from her camel;" 65 for she had said to the servant, "Who *is* this man walking in the field to meet us?" The servant said, "It *is* my master"** which she would have heard as "your husband." All she has heard was what he had (servants, flocks, riches, etc…), but now…she seems overwhelmed at how he appears. **So she took a veil and covered herself.** It seems as though only the eyes were uncovered until the union was consummated. See the story of Jacob's first night with Leah (Genesis 29:25).

my master a title all through this chapter otherwise used to refer to Abraham. Something has changed. 30 days to travel there? 30 days to travel back? This was at least two months, it seems, but Isaac is no longer the **master**'s son. In the next chapter, Abraham dies…but it's 35 more years until he does so.

Chapter 25

25:1-4

Abraham again took a wife, Apparently he got through his mourning. See more on this in 16:1-2.

25:19-20

20 Isaac was forty years old when he took Rebekah as wife, This was covered in detail in Genesis 24. **the daughter of Bethuel the Syrian** and the son of Nahor, Abraham's brother. So this Bethuel is Abraham's nephew (22:23).

of Padan Aram, we are now being prepared by the author for a flight to this location by Jacob in an episode yet to come. When we see something for the first time, we should see that we are being prepared for more information to come (such as "Canaan" in Genesis 9). **the sister of Laban the Syrian.** The word is actually "Aramaen" (see first part of verse).

25:21-22[105]

21 Isaac pleaded with the LORD for his wife What a lesson! This man maybe prayed 20 years for his **barren wife.** He is, after all, 60 years old according at the birth of the twins in 26:26.

22 But the children struggled together within her; and she said, "If all is well, why am I like this?" The pain prompts a time with the LORD.

25:23

And the LORD said to her: "Two nations are in your womb, Even 500 years later when they are thousands, perhaps hundreds of

---

[105]See also under 38:27-30.

thousands or millions of people later, they are addressed as brothers (Numbers 20:14). The LORD even appears to treat them as inheritors of separate lands (Deuteronomy 2:4-8).[106]

Two peoples shall be separated from your body; One people shall be stronger than the other, This carried forward as far as the reign of King David (2 Samuel 8:11-14). **And the older shall serve the younger."** If you received this news, how would you treat your twins? It would have been pretty hard to not have favoritism since the LORD apparently did! She simply favored the one God favored. Two chapters later, his own father made this same pronouncement, and in the New Testament Paul quotes this very verse (Romans 9:12).

Genesis 29:30-31 equates "loved less" with "hate." By comparison, Leah was loved less so much to the point where it seemed as "hate." It's a comparative term.[107] Malachi 1, furthermore says that God "hated Esau." So Rebekah only hated the one God "hated." She and God loved Jacob more. Romans 9:13 reflects this very same thought while Paul speaks of Esau/Edom who are not accounted as "children of the promise," and it had nothing to do with their merits. This is no different than the rest of the line leading to this point (Abel over Cain, Shem over Japheth, Abraham over Nahor, etc...).

25:24-26

26 Afterward his brother came out, and his hand took hold of Esau's heel; this was a very strong baby boy. **so his name was called [5]Jacob. Isaac was sixty years old when she bore them.**

---

[106]This may explain why a book about an Edomite by the name of Job made it into a Hebrew canon. This, by itself, introduces many questions for the hesitant believer ("Was their another economy of worship and acceptance with just the Edomites, etc...?")

[107]This sheds some light on Christ's admonishment in Luke 14:26.
[5]Supplanter or *Deceitful,* lit. *One Who Takes the Heel*

Since Isaac was 40 when he got married, then we are talking about almost two decades of prayer (verse 2). He could have handled it differently if he had not learned from history. His father had "improvised" and along came an older brother (by 13 years) named "Ishmael." Perhaps heartache was caused to Isaac or lessons were taught by one in the family so that Isaac didn't hurry to his own improvisation.

Incidentally, if Abraham was 100 when Isaac was born and then died at 175 years old, then these boys are 15 years old when granddad Abraham died. Maybe Abraham is wondering whether there is a plan "B" around 157 years old or so? His married son has had 17 or 18 years of marriage and it appears that he is facing the same thing that he (Abraham) was facing.

25:27-28

So the boys a **boy** was 17 in Genesis 37 so we shouldn't assume we are dealing with really young males here. **grew. And Esau was [f]a skillful hunter,** Behind Nimrod, this is the 2nd one found in this book.

25:30

And Esau said to Jacob, "Please feed me with that same red *stew,* **for I** *am* **weary." Therefore his name was called [7]Edom.** A play on **Esau** and their forefather who made a careless decision concerning food (Adam). **Edom** is equated with Esau and his descendants five times in Genesis 36.

25:31

---

[f]Gen. 27:3, 5
[7]Lit. *Red*

118

But Jacob said, "Sell me your birthright as of this day." It appears that this is different than the actual destiny from God (25:23), but maybe Isaac didn't know what God had told Rebekah? Esau sure does seem inattentive to the things that would lend themselves to running the family business—which is enormous at this time (26:27). By this time the tribe was perhaps thousands big since we have nearly 90 years since Abraham's trip to Egypt (Genesis 13) followed by his trip to Egypt (Genesis 20). A man that just loves sleeping under the stars may not be ready to be an executive.

25:32

And Esau said, "Look, I *am* about to die; I would love to think that his life was really at stake, but this seems hard to accept. If it were so, Jacob is much worse than we thought—feeding upon the desperate life of his brother.

25:34

And Jacob gave Esau bread and stew of lentils; a sort of salad-soup. After all, "stew" is added by the translators (verse 30). **then he ate and drank, arose, and went his way. Thus Esau [n]despise d *his* birthright.** He hated with what came to him by simple order of his birth, and **thus** tells us how he put this **despite** into action. Let us not forget that **Esau** was profane (Hebrews 12:16), and there is precious little pity to be had for him.

---

[n]Heb. 12:16, 17

Chapter 26

7 And the men of the place asked about his wife. And he said, "She *is* my sister" which was true for Abraham regarding Sarah (in both Genesis 12 and Genesis 20), but not so here: Isaac and **Rebekah** are 1ˢᵗ cousins, one generation removed.

8 Now it came to pass, when he had been there a long time, that Abimelech Probably nothing but a title since it means "my father is a **king."**

of the Philistines looked through a window, and saw, and there was Isaac, showing endearment to Rebekah his wife. So married folks act particularly affectionate to each other—after all, **Abimelech** didn't say, in the next verse, "quite obviously she is your favorite sister." **9 Then Abimelech called Isaac and said, "Quite obviously she *is* your wife; so how could you say, 'She *is* my sister'?"** It seems this is a different

Abimelech…hopefully…or this poor man dealth with this same scenario with **Isaac's** father (Genesis 20). We do know **Isaac** was born in Genesis 21 and he is 60 when his twins are born in Genesis 25, and they are now old enough to hunt and trick one another (last part of chapter 25). So it has been at least 75 years probably. However, there may have been lots of talk and the family may have had quite a reputation, given their size and all. Don't forget, **Isaac** owns a lot of the real estate near **Abimelech.**

Isaac said to him, "Because I said, 'Lest I die on account of her.' " People have often done things from fear (Matthew 25:25).

26:10-11

And Abimelech said, "What *is* this you have done to us? One of the people might soon have lain with your wife, that doesn't speak too well about **Abimelech**'s culture. **Might have soon lain?** Really? It happens that quickly and that loosely? And it would have been Isaac who **would have brought guilt on** these people?

26:12-16

Then Isaac sowed in that land, and reaped in the same year a hundredfold; and the LORD blessed him. Which goes well with verse 3. Apparently **Isaac** has "sojourned" long enough. **13 The man began to prosper, and continued prospering until he became very prosperous;** It looks like we are seeing fulfillment of the last part of chapter 9. We are seeing "Shem dwell in the tents of Ham." These men are, from the evidence of Genesis 10, fulfilling this prophecy of Noah's.

26:25

When did we last see an altar in Genesis where one **calls upon the name of the Lord**?

> *Genesis 12:7 And the LORD appeared unto Abram, and said, Unto thy seed will I give this land: and there builded he an altar unto the LORD, who appeared unto him. 8 he builded an altar unto the LORD, and **called upon the name of the LORD.***

So there is a reason why I'm showing you chapter 8, verse 20 and, by the way, what approach did Jesus use with the two on the road to Emmaus on the afternoon of his resurrection? Yeah, he went thematic through the whole Bible. It says, "Beginning at Moses and the prophets, he explained to them the things pertaining to himself," right? So Jesus did a thematic approach of the Scripture. Themes, he traced themes. Of course it helps when the theme is you and it also helps when you wrote the book on you so that must have been quite a Bible conference. So Jesus just traces himself all the way from Moses' books to the end, to really what was written at the time which is all the way up through Malachi.

> *Genesis 4:25 Adam knew his wife again; and she bare a son, and called his name Seth: For God, said she, hath appointed me another seed instead of Abel, whom Cain slew. And to Seth, to him also there was born a son; and he called his name Enos: then **began men to call upon the name of the LORD.***

That's the first mention of anyone "calling upon the name of the Lord." Now, let's just do a little math here and we can do this by looking at 5:3. Seth is born when Adam is how old? 130. So by the time Seth is born in chapter 4, verse 25, we are 130 years into human history and no record in the terms of Moses of anyone "calling upon the name of the Lord."

Then Seth has a son. Now, let's see here how old is Adam when Enos, the son of Seth is born? Well, we have the answer to that in 5:6

> *Seth lived **an hundred and five years**, and begat Enos.*

Alright, so we take the 130 that Adam is when Seth is born and add the 105 until Enos is born and Adam is 235 years old when men began to "call upon the name of the Lord."

We already saw Genesis 12:7, but Abraham "calls upon the name of the Lord" again in 13:4

> *Unto the place of the altar, which he had made there at the first: and there Abram **called on the name of the LORD.***

So we have Abram at the altar that he built in 12:7 doing what he did in 12:8 which is what? "Calling on the name of the Lord" at an altar and the altar presupposes that what is happening there? A sacrifice.

So we have 235 years in human history, we have the first record of anyone calling on the name of the Lord. Remember that. 12:7-8, we are now about 2,100 years in human history. We have the second person or at least the second instance of anyone **calling on the name of the Lord**. 13:4, we have Abram going to the same altar that he built, offering a sacrifice, calling on the name of the Lord.

Look at Acts 9. When you look at the first few verses of Acts 9, what's the event? Conversion of Saul who is also known as Paul, alright? We find Christ speaking, in verse 15, to Ananias in verse 10: the Lord appears to Ananias and the Lord says to him in a vision, "Ananias. And he said, Behold, I am here," and he tells us Ananias in Damascus, "Go and find Paul." And Ananias says in verse 13, "I have heard by many of this man, how much evil he hath done to thy saints at Jerusalem: And here he hath authority from the chief priests to bind," look here, **all that call on thy name.**

If **calling upon the name of the Lord** means to ask God to save you, we have a problem. Let me give you a list of the problems so far. 1. You have nobody getting saved for almost 200 years of human history. 2. Abraham is offering a sacrifice, calling on the name of the Lord, and we don't know what he's calling on and we don't know what he's asking for. We don't have any idea contextually what he's asking for. Now, there is a reason why I am saying it this way because in Romans 10:13, when you ask someone "Are you saved?"

"Yes, I'm saved."

"How do you know you're saved?"

"Yes, I know I'm saved."

123

"Why do you know you're saved?"

So how do you know you're saved? "Well, I asked God to save me." "Well, how do you know that God saves when you ask him to save you?" And almost, I wish I could give a nickel for every time that I could predict this answer, "Well, because the Bible says for whosoever shall call on the name of the Lord shall be saved." Well, it does. It says it in Genesis 4, Genesis 12, Genesis 13, Joel 2 and Acts 9. Now, if it means to ask God to save you, let's understand what the Lord is saying, what Ananias said in verse 14, "And here he hath authority from the chief priests to arrest everyone who asks Jesus into their heart." Oops. That's not in there. Well, what if it means to ask God to save them? "And here he hath authority from the chief priests to bind or arrest everyone who asks God to save them." Whoops, that's not in there either.

So the question you have to ask yourself is: what did that phrase mean? In Acts 9:15-21, for example: did it really mean that Paul was waiting around for people to "say the prayer" so he could arrest them?

> *1 Corinthians 1:1 Paul, called to be an apostle of Jesus Christ through the will of God, and Sosthenes our brother, Unto the church of God which is at Corinth, to them that are sanctified in Christ Jesus, called to be saints, with all that in every place **call upon the name of Jesus Christ our Lord.***

Wait a minute, now Paul is saying that you can identify the believers in Corinth because they continually do something. What do they continually do according to the Scripture? "Call on the name of the Lord." What did Abraham continually do? What did Isaac continually do?

So you can't take a phrase that is used 100 times in the Bible and pick one in Romans 10 and make it mean "ask to be saved." Do you see how inconsistent that is? It hasn't meant that anytime before Romans 10 and it doesn't mean that anytime after Romans 10 but we say it means that in Romans 10. Now think about that. There are 39 Old Testament books and it is never meant to ask Jesus into your heart or to ask God to save you. Not once. But in Romans 10 it does? Remember, salvation in John 3:16 is "believing in him and not perishing but having everlasting life."

In 1 Corinthians 1:2, if it meant "asking God to come into your heart," think about the nonsense that verse would be communicating. Every Sunday we get together and "we ask God to come into our hearts, we ask God to save us." Do you believe Abraham had to get saved every time he offered a sacrifice? So that can't be what the phrase means.

If people started doing it when a certain man was born, Enos, Genesis 4, 235 years in human history; If Abraham did it and did it numerous times and only did it when he worshiped; and Isaac did it and did it numerous times and did it particularly when he worshiped, and Paul would find those people that normally did it and arrest them, and he identified people that met every Lord's day, 1 Corinthians 1, as those who did it, it must be an act of worship. It must be the act of worshiping God.

So if you want to read Romans 10:13 with the backdrop we just added to it, you could say it this way: "the ones that worship God are the ones that are saved. You want to identify people that are saved? Find the worshipers of God."

26:25-26

And he builded an altar there, and called upon the name of the LORD, and pitched his tent there: and there Isaac's servants digged a well. Then Abimelech went to him from Gerar, and Ahuzzath one of his friends, and Phichol, The chief captain of his army. So here's Abimelech who had a run-in earlier in the

125

chapter, and he chased Isaac off of the wells. We've already seen that. Abimelech is now not the favorite guy in the land. He shows up with this guy named **Phichol**, alright?

Ahuzzath, one of his friends. Now, this is the first time Ahuzzath is mentioned in the Old Testament, in the Bible, so I don't think that there's anything other than a record here being placed for something future that occurs, but this Phichol guy, he occurs at another part of Scripture.

> *21:22 it came to pass at that time, that Abimelech and* **Phichol** *the chief captain of his host spake unto Abraham, saying, God is with thee in all that thou doest.*

So we could be dealing with a man here that is giving insight to the successive leader with the title Abimelech in chapter 26. It could be "Look, this is Isaac, the son of Abraham, be careful what you're doing here." I could be.

26:27-28

28 they said, We saw certainly that the LORD was with thee. This is a clear indication that God blessed Isaac right in front of Abimelech and maybe at the time he didn't realize that it was God's blessing until Isaac left with the blessing and then all of a sudden Abimelech's house is not flourishing, his crops aren't growing, his animals aren't growing, they're not breeding like they were and things are not as good as when Isaac was in town. That could be.

and we said, Let there be now an oath betwixt us, even betwixt us and thee, Who was really behind this whole well thing? They dug a well that Abraham had, Isaac and his people dug wells that Abraham had and they were chased out of there. The folks of Abimelech came up and said, "Hey, this is our water," so they went off and dug another well. They said, "This is our water." They went off and dug another well. Before you know it, they're out of town and so Abimelech says, "Why have you left?" And Isaac says, "Why are you coming to see me, seeing that you hate me?"

Who did Isaac see behind this? Abimelech. Well, that makes the comments of the next verse a little funnier.

and let us make a covenant with thee. "Let us make a covenant together." Who made the first covenant? Abraham and God. Seven animals cut in half, split, and typically in that part of the world, the parties of the covenant would walk between the two animals—the two sections of animals. Basically the idea was, "If I break my promise to you, may I be like one of these animals, severed in half." The second covenant that involved cutting was circumcision. Probably, then, it's realistic that when Abimelech and Isaac made a covenant that they would leave each other alone, it's realistic that they also severed animals and walked between them. At the end of verse 31, they found a well. Verse 32, "And it came to pass the same day, that Isaac's servants came, and told him concerning the well which they had digged, and said unto him, We have found water. And he called it Shebah: therefore the name of the city is Beersheba unto this day." Now, Beersheba comes from a couple Hebrew words and the Hebrew words mean "the oath of seven." So probably this "Beersheba" and the one prior to this were named at places where covenants were made, particularly seven animals were severed and the parties of these covenants would walk. That's Genesis 15 and Genesis 26.

26:29

That thou wilt do us no hurt. I have to tell you I'm a little humored here. His people ran Isaac off from their wells and then Abimelech chases them and says, "Look, I can tell you are blessed of God. Can we agree not to pick on each other anymore?"

as we have not touched thee, and as we have done unto thee

127

nothing but good, and have sent thee away in peace. This is like punching someone in the mouth and then putting your hand out and saying, "We're cool, aren't we?" It's really amusing, actually and so I would be asking if I were Isaac, "You treated me right? You sent me away in peace?"

26:30

he made them a feast, and they did eat and drink. So there is a dinner happening here. It's amazing what you can get people to say around a dinner table. So have we seen this supper before? Have we seen any meals in the book of Genesis before? Chapter 18, three men, and one of them was God. Two of them were the angels that performed the snatch and grab with Lot and his girls there in Sodom. We find that when the angels visited Sodom, and it says that he made them a meal. In 21:8, we have a meal to celebrate Isaac's weaning. In chapter 24 when we have Eliezer bargaining for the hand of Rebekah for Isaac. Yeah, so there's a meal there.

26:31-32[108]

26:33

So he called it [7]Shebah. Therefore the name of the city *is* [8]Beers heba to this day. Again, this was already named such by Moses earlier in the book (21:33). Another possibility is that this is a 2nd well with the same name.

26:34-35

When Esau was forty years old, Let's remind ourselves that Exodus 12:40, along with 1 Kings 6:1, with a secular date of 966 B.C. for the building of Solomon's temple we have an approximate

---

[108]See notes on 26:27-28.
[7]Lit. *Oath* or *Seven*
[8]Lit. *Well of the Oath* or *Well of the Seven*

date by simply adding 25 years between the start of the 430 years (in Abraham's 75[109] year in Genesis 12)[109] mentioned in Exodus 12:40 and Isaac's birth, the 60 years of Isaac's life that pass before Esau's birth and now these **forty years** to get an approximate date of 1751 B.C.

he took as wives Judith the daughter of Beeri the Hittite, and Basemath the daughter of Elon These marriages are discussed more in Genesis 36, and we see that Ishmael is involved as well. Yet another concern. **the Hittite.** The reader must take note of the last verse of the next chapter and see my note there. **35 And they were a grief of mind to Isaac and Rebekah.** He married two Hittites, and it irritated his parents. So much that Genesis 28 shows us their sending Jacob off to be sure he did not do the same (along with their fear of Esau's retribution).

One reason for this grief—other than their paganism—is that they are promised death (Genesis 15:18-20.

---

[109]Which gives us a date of 1876 B.C. for Abraham's 75th year. At this point we use the genealogies of Genesis 5 and Genesis 11 to get a date of creation.

Chapter 27

27:2-4

Then he said, "Behold now, I am old. I ^cdo not know the day of my death. If Esau is still 40 here then we have no doubt that Isaac lives another 80 years! Even if this is closer to what will be found as the departure of Jacob near his 80th birthday Isaac still lives another 40 years! What declining health! On the other hand, Abraham lives another 35 years after Isaac gets married and Isaac is already taking over the family business which means that Abraham feels quite old.

27:15

Then Rebekah took the choice clothes of her elder son Esau, which *were* with her in the house, and put them on Jacob her younger son. We need to remember these boys are at least 40 years old.

27:20

But Isaac said to his son, "How *is it* that you have found *it* so quickly, my son?" And he said, "Because the LORD your God brought *it* to me." It is significant that this is the only time that one refers to "your God" in the book of Genesis.[110] Was this on account of the shame he felt or did he feel some measure of distance from **God?**

27:24

---

^cProv. 27:1; James 4:14

[110]"KJV Search Results for "thy god"." Blue Letter Bible. Web. 16 Nov, 2018.
<https://www.blueletterbible.org//search/search.cfm?Criteria=%22thy+god%22&t=KJV#s=s_primary_0_1>.

130

Then he said, "*Are* you really my son Esau?" He said, "I *am*." His 3rd lie in this episode.

27:29

Let peoples serve you, And nations bow down to you. Which Jacob, in turn, says about Judah (Genesis 49:10).

27:37

Then Isaac answered and said to Esau, "Indeed I have made him your master, Nevermind that it was a blessing that wasn't intended for **Jacob;** it was binding. This reminds us of the promise of Joshua to the Gibeonites (Joshua 9:1-9; 2 Samuel 21:1-2) which was binding even though it was misspoken, and we find application in things as simple as marriage vows that "weren't a good idea."

27:46

And Rebekah said to Isaac, "I am weary of my life because of the daughters of Heth; ˢif Jacob takes a wife of the daughters of Heth, This is exactly 26:34's point and probably the opposing end of this section. In other words, what we read in between the two mentionings may be related to the two. Or, the reason we know what transpired between 26:34 and here is because of how much grief Esau's choice of wife brought to his mother. **like these *who are* the daughters of the land, what good will my life be to me?"** Whatever consternation Rebekah has concerning Esau's choice of women we have to remember it was exacerbated by the word she received from the Lord (Genesis 25:23). Did she feel as though she felt like she was supposed to help fulfill it?

ˢGen. 24:3

Chapter 28[111]

28:10-14[112]

As you might expect, we have an account of God reaching down to man through a ladder in juxtaposition to the men who built a tower to get to God (Genesis 11:1-9).

13 And behold, the LORD stood above it Other than Jacob here, Abraham and Isaac are the only other people to whom God shows Himself (Genesis 15, 17, 18;) while Abimelech is the only other person to hear from God in a dream (Genesis 20).

14 Also your descendants shall be as the dust of the earth; you shall spread abroad to the west and the east, to the north and the south; and in you and in your seed all the families of the earth shall be blessed. First given to his grandfather (Genesis 12:3-7). Galatians 3:8 speaks of this as the Christ plan. Isaiah 9:1-7 speaks of other nations being in God's plan at least as far back as Isaiah's ministry. Shortly later, we have Zechariah 14 speaking of "all families" in the future to attend feasts in Jerusalem. Revelation 22 speaks now of the "nations" coming to eat of the fruit of the tree of life for healing.

28:18-22[113]

Then Jacob rose early in the morning, Just as Abraham did on the morning that he sent Ishmael away (Genesis 21:14) and the day that he arose to take Isaac away to sacrifice (Genesis 22:1)

and took the stone that he had put at his head, set it up as a pillar Genesis 31:13 finds a reminder that this episode is called an "anointing" **and poured oil** The first time **oil** is used in Scripture[114]

---

[111]See also introduction & 2:1-3.
[112]See also under 28:18-22.
[113]See my commentary on Luke (9:18-36).
[114]"Genesis 28:13 (KJV) - And behold the LORD stood." Blue Letter

on top of it. This is, then, the first place in Scripture where something is "anointed with **oil.**" In other words, all future revelation concerning this topic comes here for a starting point. It is here from which all understanding flourishes. Genesis 31:13, then, is the first place this form of the noun "Messiah" (English transliteration) is found,[115] and thus it is the beginning of our understanding of the New Testament equivalent for "Christ."

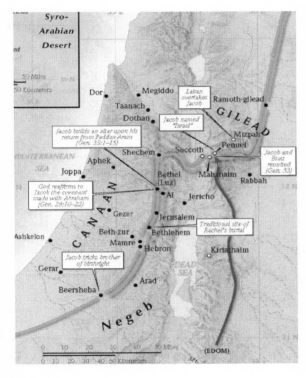

19 And he called the name of that place Bethel; See map. I am afraid I wasn't thinking about publishing when I cropped this map and if I find the source I will cite it here immediately for future printings/revisions.

but the name of that city had been Luz previously. "almond" became "House of God." When God shows up in a place, it becomes very special.

...the idea of a divine passageway to heaven from earth

Bible. Web. 8 Oct, 2019.
<https://www.blueletterbible.org/kjv/gen/28/13/t_conc_28018>.
    [115]"Genesis 31:13 (KJV) - I am the God of." Blue Letter Bible. Web. 8 Oct, 2019. <https://www.blueletterbible.org/kjv/gen/31/13/t_conc_31013>.

was familiar to the ancients. The name "Babylon" means "gate of the god(s)" (*bāb-ili; bāb-ilāni*; see vol. 1A, p. 469), indicating the entryway to the deity's presence or the place of divine judgment.[116]

Know that this is the place where God can be encountered, and we know that God is encountered through Christ (John 1:51; 14:6). The only difference between "almonds" and "house of God" is God revealing Himself to a human being. This special place of oil anointing, then, is seen differently when it is given to God. In other words, identities change when you meet at a place that is anointed with oil.

21 so that I come back to my father's house in peace, then this first "anointing with oil" episode, then accompanies a covenant that shall be made with God. **the LORD shall be my God.** This is a place where vows are made and agreements struck between two parties. When Jacob saw Bethel; when he saw the pillar; he saw a place where he had made an agreement with God.

22 And this stone which I have set as a pillar shall be God's house, and of all that You give me I will surely give a tenth to You." There are Covenantal,[117] Historical,[118] Sensible,[119] and Biblical. An overcommitted 90% is the real issue more than an undersized 100%. Wealth, anyway, is not what one needs but how little one needs. Jacob learned how to tithe, probably, from his

---

[116]K. A. Mathews, *Genesis 11:27–50:26*, vol. 1B, The New American Commentary (Nashville: Broadman & Holman Publishers, 2005), 453.

[117]If you have a covenant church membership, there is a strong probability that "tithing" is a part of the church's statement of faith or church covenant. If you don't agree, don't join.

[118]Since the first century, Jewish believers made an easy transition between Saturday Sabbath worship and Sunday, first-day-of-worship which included reading, exposition, and…tithing.

[119]If the church has property, caretakers, staff, utilities, equipment…somebody needs to think about paying for it; this could be said about pastoral support, benevolence giving, and missions support as well.

grandfather Abraham (Genesis 14:20). This was a promise in response to the promise God had already made to him (verses 13-15). This is pre-Mosaic by 400 years. In other words, long before the first priest of Moses' law, God fearers were offering tithes.

Chapter 29

29:1-3

So Jacob went on his journey and came to the land of the people of the East. Probably the same geography, then, as the episode in 11:1-2. Many maps say, then, that **Jacob** traveled in excess of 400 miles to get to this "well" of verse 2.

29:4

And Jacob said to them, "My brethren, three of them (verse 2)?

29:7

Then he said, "Look, *it is* still ¹high day; *it is* not time for the cattle to be gathered together. Water the sheep, and go and feed *them*." A pretty audacious Jacob. We're not surprised here, but this does speak of his agricultural expertise.

29:8

But they said, "We cannot until all the flocks are gathered together, and they It's hard to ascertain who this is. Maybe there was a ranking shepherd that comes last and owns the well or is the president of the co-op? **have rolled the stone from the well's mouth;** It's hard to know why they had to wait.

29:9-12

12 And Jacob told Rachel that he *was* her father's relative Genesis 24:15 helps us with how these two are related. If **Jacob's** father is Isaac and **Jacob's** mother is **Laban's** sister, then **Jacob** is currently talking to his first cousin. So **Jacob** is **Rachel's father's** nephew. Funny thing: even though Laban is **Jacob's** uncle, they

---

¹early in the day

are also 2nd cousins (sharing the same great grandfather (Terah: 1. Father of Abraham, **Jacob's** grandfather; 2. Father of Nahor, Laban's grandfather).

and that he *was* Rebekah's son. ^kSo she ran and told her father. We saw this almost exactly with her aunt reacted in chapter 24.

29:13

Then it came to pass, when Laban heard the report about Jacob his sister's son, that he ran to meet him, maybe **Laban** loved his extended family…but the last time they had a visitor from Abraham's side it meant riches to their own family.

and embraced him and kissed him, and brought him to his house. How long has it been since this **Laban** saw Rebekah, his sister, leave? Well, Jacob is no less than 40 years old (last verses of Genesis 25) while he was born 20 years into his mother and father's marriage. So it has been 60 years since these two branches of the same family have seen one another (as far as we know).

29:15-17

Then Laban said to Jacob, "Because you are my relative, should you therefore serve me Jacob would have been fine working among flocks. It's hard to find people who are low profile.

17 Leah's eyes were delicate, but Rachel was beautiful of form and appearance. They must have been similar in size or Jacob would have known something was amiss. What we can say here is that **Rachel** was shapely, and **Leah** had **delicate eyes.** Quite the strange contrast. The veil was probably over most of every face in these situations thus requiring descriptions of

---

^kGen. 24:28

137

Leah's eyes.

In regards to wine, Genesis 9, 19, 24 (if Rebekah's dad is hung over in the last morning of that episode), and in this chapter may have been an impairer of judgment.

29:20

So Jacob served seven years for Rachel, and they seemed only a few days to him because of the love he had for her. There is no hint that **Rachel** knew her dad was going to pull this "cultural norm." 31:26 shows us that Laban was consistently conniving.

29:24-28[120]

And Laban gave his maid Zilpah to his daughter Leah as a maid. After Hagar, **Zilpah** is the second **maid** in the book of Genesis. **25 So it came to pass in the morning, that behold, it was Leah.** I try not to quote other authors en mass, but this was too good to pass up:

> *Jacob stays in love seven years (vs. 20), and the 2,520 days seem like "a few days" (vs. 20) because of the dreamlike trance that he is in.* One can see him mooning around the ranch like a sick cow, writing sonnets, and soliloquizing to the moon and stars at night, and occasionally serenading Rachel under her balcony. The mood is captured well in the conversation of the newlyweds who were strolling on the beach at Miami (on their honeymoon). The reception constitutes the ceremony, and the father takes his daughter to the prospective groom. It is 8 p.m. (or near there) the last night of the feast, and Jacob goes back to his tent, alone as usual. An hour later there is the sound of slippered feet in the sand outside, and with his heart nearly jumping up into

---

[120]See also under 38:12-16.

his mouth, Jacob goes to the front flap to receive his beloved. He has waited 2,520 nights for this night, and now it has arrived! In the moonlight stands the veiled figure of his heart's affections, and beside her "giving the bride away" is Laban (who never gave anything away). Very few words are exchanged, and if "Rachel" said anything, it must have been with some effort. Jacob attributes her incoherence to "stage fright" or "honeymoon heebie-jeebies." For Laban, *in this instance, "silence is truly golden." Jacob bids his father-in-law "good night," and* almost knocks "Rachel" down hustling her into the tent. Laban goes home whistling "There's a Gold Mine in the Sky, Bye and Bye," and everyone is happy. That is, until morning (vs. 25)...Leah keeps her mouth shut (except for kisses) and passes off as the *bride elect. But "in the morning, behold, it was Leah!!" (vs. 25). Jacob sleeps late, opens* his eyes at 9 a.m., yawns, smiles to himself, snuggles into the pillow with happy memories, and reaches over to put his arm around his beloved. He yawns and smiles again to himself, thinking of the wonderful night and the wonderful days and nights to *follow. "Rachel" yawns and stretches, rolls over, and...! Oh, good night, nurse! It's the* wrong woman!![121]

And he said to Laban, "What is this you have done to me? Was it not for Rachel that I served you? Why then have you deceived me?" Did Jacob forget chapters 26-27 and what it was like to **deceive** somebody? Hosea 8:7 speaks of "sowing in the wind and reaping in the whirlwind." Probably, now, Jacob knows how his brother felt after being swindled from his blessing.

26 And Laban said, "It must not be done so in our country,

---

[121]Ruckman, Dr. Peter S.. Genesis Commentary (The Bible Believer's Commentary Series) (Kindle Locations 11625-11650). BB Bookstore. Kindle Edition.

"I'm just going according to custom." Laban could have told him this before. **to give the younger before the firstborn.** After Jacob had, 20 years earlier, partaken in the "switcharoo" that his mother played on his father regarding the son who needed to be blessed (Genesis 27), he "reaped" (Galatians 6:7-9) by getting "okeedoked" into getting a woman in his bed other than the one he expected. **27 Fulfill her week, and we will give you this one also for the service which you will serve with me still another seven years."** Imagine how Leah felt during this time. She wasn't chosen by anything but culture!

28 Then Jacob did so and fulfilled her week. In the Hebrew this really only means "fulfill her seven." Sometimes a **week** in Scripture is seven years (Daniel 9). It need not be that here.

If **her** is Rachel, then it could be another **week** of years. However, if **her** is Leah, then it could mean a **week** of days. Judges 14 gives us light here. Verses 10 and 11 show us that there were marriage feasts that lasted 7 days. Or, to say it this way, a **week** of days was the length of a marriage feast. This is, no doubt, the meaning here in Genesis. So Jacob marries twice in two weeks' time. He paid, therefore, for one before he got her, and he paid for the other after he got her (Rachel). 30:1, then, takes place after Rachel watches her sister give Jacob four sons right away.

29:31-33

When the LORD saw that Leah was unloved,[122] translated "hated" in other versions. This helps us understand some N.T. verses like Romans 9:13...Esau was "unloved" or "loved less" and in the Gospels, Jesus requires us to "love wives, etc.... less" (versus "hate"). **He opened her womb; but Rachel was barren.**

---

[122]Lit. *hated*

140

It is the LORD Who gives children. Psalm 127 makes it appear that children are actually a blessing from God. **32 So Leah conceived and bore a son, and she called his name** We have no clue that Leah consulted her husband on what to name these boys. His influence was plenty clear.

33 Then she conceived again and bore a son, and said, "Because the LORD has heard that I am unloved,[123] She has a measure of faith, to be sure. She thinks God cares about her! In the last of this chapter, we find four sons...all of them named after how Leah feels about her relationship with her husband. All of them, addressed in like order by Jacob some 50 years later and having blessing pronounced or denounced in Genesis 49.

29:35

And she conceived again and bore a son, and said, "Now I will praise the LORD." Therefore she called his name Judah.[9] It means to "praise/confess with extended hands."

---

[123]Lit. *hated*
[9]Lit. *Praise*

Chapter 30

30:1[124]

30:2

And Jacob's anger was aroused against Rachel, and he said, "*Am* I in the place of God, who has withheld from you the fruit of the womb?" "Woman! I am doing everything I can!" (we know what he meant). But this does sound like a great line from the actual hero of Genesis (50:19).

30:3-6

So she said, "Here is ᵉmy maid Bilhah; go in to her, and she will bear *a child* on my knees, that I also may have children by her." Means exactly what it says. This is a cultural practice where the barren woman would have her surrogate giver birth on her (the barren woman's) lap so that it was symbolized that the child would be counted as hers (the barren woman's).

6 Then Rachel said, "God has judged my case; and He has also heard my voice and given me a son." Therefore she called his name ²Dan. Which means **Dan**iel means "judged by God."

30:9

When Leah saw that she it seems that we are talking about Bilhah, and so we have an adjusted timeline—unless, of course **she** is **Leah** (in which case **Zilpah** and Bilhah are having children around the same time in years 8-14 of Jacob's working relationship with Laban).

---

[124]30:1-9 is discussed somewhat in 16:1-2.
ᵉGen. 16:2
²Lit. *Judge*

30:11

Then Leah said, "A troop comes!" So she called his name [6]Gad. Hoping for this to be the "first of many?" This makes good sense that Rachel's firstborn in the hopes of the "first of many" when we consider the meaning of Joseph.

There is a possibility that they are fearing Esau's eventual revenge.

30:15

But she said to her, "*Is it* a small matter that you have taken away my husband? Would you take away my son's mandrakes also?" the Greeks call this "love apple." **And Rachel said, "Therefore he will lie with you tonight for your son's mandrakes."** So a trade is taking place: the "love apple" for a night with the husband. It seems, then, that this **mandrake** may have aided with fertility.

30:16

When Jacob came out of the field in the evening, Leah went out to meet him and said, "You must come in to me, for I have surely hired you with my son's mandrakes." And he lay with her that night. The implication is that **Jacob** would not have **come into** her had she not **hired** him (presumably away from Rachel). It seems in all this, then, that Jacob and Leah stopped "being together", given the last phrase of 29:35.

30:18-20

Leah said, "God has given me my wages, because I have given my maid to my husband." So she called his name [8]Issachar.

---

[6]Lit. *Troop* or *Fortune*
[8]Lit. *Wages*

More sad stuff about the relationship with her husband and the inability to compete with her pretty sister (who is also her sister in law by marriage).

20 And Leah said, "God has endowed me *with* a good endowment; now my husband will dwell with me, because I have borne him six sons." So she called his name [9]Zebulun. More sad story: "Maybe now my husband will be pleased to "be" with me.

30:22-23

Then God [o]remembered Rachel, covenantal language or "language of intent" much like 8:1.

23 And she conceived and bore a son, and said, "God has taken away [q]my reproach." Much like Hannah (1 Samuel 1) and Elizabeth (Luke 1) will say.

30:27

And Laban said to him, "Please *stay,* if I have found favor in your eyes, *for* I have learned by experience There is some evidence in the Hebrew that this is "divining" or mystical acts **that the LORD has blessed me for your sake."**

30:30

For what you had before I *came was* little, and it has increased to a great amount; the LORD has blessed you since my coming. And now, when shall I also provide for my own house?" "All I have in my wallet is a library card after working for you for these 20 years!"

---

[9]Lit. *Dwelling*
[o]Gen. 19:29; 1 Sam. 1:19, 20
[q]1 Sam. 1:6; Luke 1:25

30:31-32

So he said, "What shall I give you?" And Jacob said, "You shall not give me anything. The next phrases indicates that **Jacob** may have given this some thought—given the speed of his response.

32 Let me pass through all your flock today, removing from there all the speckled and spotted sheep, and all the brown ones among the lambs, and the spotted and speckled among the goats; The Hebrews seems to say "she-goats."

30:36

Then he put three days' journey between himself and Jacob, This would ensure that the wages of **Jacob** would not be bloated by wandering flocks. Thankfully, the cousins of **Jacob fed the rest of Laban's flocks** far enough away that they would not see what was about to happen.

30:38

And the rods which he had peeled, he set before the flocks in the gutters, in the watering troughs where the flocks came to drink, so that they should conceive when they came to drink. If mandrakes work with humans, then I guess I am not surprised there are ways to manipulate animals also.

30:41

And it came to pass, whenever the stronger livestock conceived, that Jacob placed the rods before the eyes of the livestock in the gutters, that they might conceive among the rods. So get all the animals that have the marks and then make more that have the marks. These were the two goals of **Jacob.** He

145

was so good at it that the cousins saw they were losing just about everything (31:1).

Chapter 31

31:13[125]

31:24

But God had come to Laban the Syrian in a dream by night, and said to him, "Be careful that you speak to Jacob neither good nor bad." Abraham (Genesis 15), Abimelech (Genesis 20), Jacob (Genesis 28) and Jacob (Genesis 32) make this the 5th **dream.** Incidentally, the 400 years of captivity promised to Abraham leads to dreams which lead to the deliverer Moses in the next book while 400 years of "captivity" after Malachi preceded **dreams** (Matthew 1) which preceded Jesus' first coming and **dreams** are promised before His 2nd Coming (Joel 2; Acts 2).

31:29

It is in my power to do you harm, but the God of your father It is interesting that Laban's daddy didn't have the same **God,** while their great grandfather Terah had heard from the Lord (Genesis 11:31-12:1).[126] Nahor, then, was the breakdown of Laban's spiritual heritage. It didn't have to be simply **your father.** The fact that Laban has idols that Rachel could steal (verse 32) is indicative of a problem already. It should be pointed out that 117 years have passed since **Laban** and his parents sent Jacob's mother to his **father** (20 years of childlessness, plus 77 years of age Jacob was at time of his fleeing from Esau, plus 20 years of working for **Laban).**

31:35

---

[125]See under 28:18-22.

[126]The word "had" found in 12:1 means that God had discussed the matter with Abraham, but the preceding verses in chapter 11 show that Terah made the journey as well.

And she said to her father, "Let it not displease my lord that I cannot [h]rise before you as is custom, and still should be. for the manner of women *is* with me." Lady sickness, thus making the saddle unclean? Possible menstral pain? Both of these are decent ideas.

31:38

These twenty years I *have been* with you; your ewes and your female goats have not miscarried their young, an exaggeration?

31:44

Now therefore, come, [q]let us make a covenant, you and I, and let it be a witness between you and me." This is quite a conundrum, having—in his words—lost his flocks and daughters and their maidservants; having chased them all for the last (figuratively speaking) week. His mood has seemingly been changed and he is now ready to be civil.

---

[h]Lev. 19:32
[q]Gen. 21:27, 32; 26:28

Chapter 32

32:1

So Jacob went on his way, and the angels of God met him. So Jacob has been gone 20 years finding wives and wealth. Laban has finally resigned himself that Jacob and family are not returning to Haran. Here **the angels of God met him.** The last time Jacob saw angels, they were moving up and down on the staircase to Heaven in Genesis 28. It has been about 20 years since he has seen them at Bethel ("House of God"). **Angels of God** is found in only these two places in Genesis.

32:2

When Jacob saw them, he said, "This is God's camp." And he called the name of that place Mahanaim. Or "double camp." If you ever see a word ending in "im," it's probably the Hebrew plural. Think of "Baalim" as in Isaiah 66, for example ("more than one Baal") or "seraphim" (Isaiah 6). It must, therefore, mean that there are two camps of Jacob's people.

32:3

Then Jacob sent messengers before him to Esau his brother in the land of Seir, the country of Edom. The last time we saw this guy, he was marrying people that were not in the approval of his parents. This lifestyle is both the cause and the result of Isaac and Rebekah's sending of Jacob to another land, the land of their relatives, to get a wife. Yes, Esau married ungodly, non-covenant people twice.

Interestingly enough, **Seir** meaning "hairy" and **Edom** refer to Esau. Remember, **Edom** was a result of his sinning over food, or giving away the grace of God over food as Adam did. Moses is perhaps adding this additional light and that **the country of Edom**[127] is really called something else some 400 years previous to authorship.

Remember that Job is from this very place, more specifically the land of "Uz." Lamentations 4:21 tells us this "Uz" is in "Edom." Job, therefore, is from this same place of Edom.

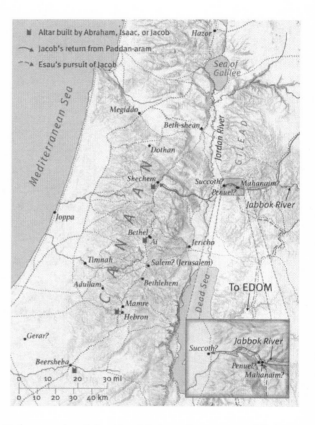

32:4

And he commanded them, saying, "Speak thus to my lord Esau, 'Thus your servant Jacob says: "I have dwelt with Laban and stayed there until now. In other words, "please give him the history lesson, and how we got to this place."

---

[127]The picture was procured while preparing the class wherein I taught this material. I pray I can re-locate the source of the picture by and by in order to give proper credit for future editions of this commentary.

32:5

I have oxen, donkeys, flocks, and male and female servants; and I have sent to tell my lord, Jacob is establishing himself as the subordinate.

32:7

So Jacob was greatly afraid and distressed; Yes, how would you feel if a guy you saw 20 years ago was angry—very angry—with you was approaching you with tokens of his own prosperity: 400 men? Esau has found a way to be prosperous also. We're not told about how this happened. If we do all the surmising here that we do with Abraham (318 men with families, probably), we are seeing a man with at least that much. What if he had that much assumed wealth as well? Esau was a mighty man!

32:8

And he said, "If Esau comes to the one company and attacks it, then the other company which is left will escape." Who gets to be in the "other group" which could be decimated, perhaps? He has the promise of his father Isaac that he would be blessed with many seed to inherit the promised land (Genesis 28:12ff). So somebody, theoretically, must survive. He is not at home yet.

32:10

I am not worthy of the least of all the mercies and of all the truth which You have shown Your servant; for I crossed over this Jordan with my staff, and now I have become two companies. I left with a stick and now have two camps!

32:11

Deliver me, I pray, from the hand of my brother, from the

hand of Esau; for I fear him, lest he come and attack me and the mother with the children. A crisis of faith! He's already been promised that he would live through this! See the next verse.

32:12

For You said, 'I will surely treat you well, and make your descendants as the sand of the sea, which cannot be numbered for multitude.'" Twice, this frightened Jacob reminds God of his promise that he and his would receive a certain land. God had promised his grandfather Abraham in Genesis 22 and his father Isaac in Genesis 26. Later, he promised this same Jacob in chapter 28. "I'm afraid, and it doesn't hurt to remind God of His promise." Maybe this is simply Jacob desiring to take interest in God's promise. After having left dad 450 miles behind, Jacob is now interested in reuniting with his father. Statements later in the book tell us that Jacob was approximately 77 when he left Isaac. This would have made Isaac 137 years old. Isaac is still alive, then, as he dies at 180 years old and he is currently 157 years old.

If Isaac is still at Beersheeba, his boys are about to tangle about 100 miles from home. Jacob probably feels like the third wheel as Mount Seir is only about 50 miles from dad.

32:13

So he lodged there that same night, and took what came to his hand as a present for Esau his brother: He has already split his things/people into two groups, but he doesn't feel like that is enough.

32:15

thirty milk camels with their colts, forty cows and ten bulls, twenty female donkeys and ten foals. That should just about satisfy anybody.

152

32:16

Then he delivered them to the hand of his servants, every drove by itself, and said to his servants, "Pass over before me, and put some distance between successive droves." Maybe Esau will sit and think "What should I do with all of these animals?"

32:19-20

So he commanded the second, the third, and all who followed the droves, So there were more than the four groups. This makes sense later in the next chapter when both brothers say "I have enough." Clearly, Jacob has some behind the three groups if he can still say "Take these from me; I have enough."

20 and also say, 'Behold, your servant For the third time in this passage, Jacob wants his people to let Esau know that he knows he is at the mercy of Esau. "Jacob, your servant, your minion, your boot-licker…is behind us. **Jacob is behind us.' " For he said, "I will appease** "You're going to stall. Basically, you're going to buy me time and earn me some mercy. Maybe I'll survive, but hopefully somebody will." The word here is *kippur* which means he was hoping for there to be an atonement of sorts. **him with the present that goes before me, and afterward I will see his face; perhaps he will accept me."** This is not how it actually transpires in the next chapter. Jacob goes before them, "bowing 7 times" and then as he is talking to Esau, the droves come up behind them one by one. Jacob has changed the plan a few times here.

32:21

So the present went on over before him, So there was a Jabbok crossing and a Jordan crossing in this story. Many think this was a play on words on "Jacob." Don't forget this was a potentially huge tangle in the wilderness so this is not out of the question that this encounter was of such magnitude that they just named the river after the event. **but he himself lodged that night in the camp.**

32:22

And he arose that night and took his two wives, his two female servants, and his eleven sons, and crossed over the ford of Jabbok. The order of march is spelled out in the next chapter, first few verses. It is rather humorous. We hope they don't all die....but if they do, let's have a preferred order of death. Leah is going to get a very clear signal that she is not the favorite with Leah bringing up the rear. **Jabbok** is probably playing on the name "Jacob."

32:23-31a

24 Then Jacob was left alone; and a Man wrestled Hosea 12 indicates this was "an angel."[128] The only reason we know it's an Angel is because Hosea said so. **with him until the breaking of day.**

25 Now when He saw that He did not prevail against him, He touched the socket of his hip; and the socket of Jacob's hip was out of joint as He wrestled with him. One must wonder what God is teaching Jacob in this his second recorded wrestling match (the first of which being with his brother in chapter 26).

26 And ˣHe said, "Let Me go, for the day breaks." This is a testament to his strength, much like his moving the stone on the well in chapter 31. Really, think about how well an infant can grab and grasp another person's foot. Jacob could.

But he said, "I will not let You go So "wrestling" could be simply

---

[128]The same angel he saw in chapter 28 at Bethel.
ˣ Luke 24:28

defined as hanging onto a garment with desperation. **unless You bless me!"** Again, Hosea 12 says he wept as well. Moreover, Hosea 12 says there was much "waiting" in this episode. This, by the way, is a hint that Jacob knew he was wrestling a heavenly angel. You don't usually ask an adversary to **bless** you.

27 So He said to him, "What is your name?" He said, "Jacob." Do you remember Genesis 27, Isaac asked him "Who are you," and Jacob lied. Here is a moment which throws Jacob back to a moment of honesty. It seems, then, that this wrestling match serves as a reminder of what it means to cause turmoil in the life of another person. Moreover, Jacob thinks that his biggest need here is safety from Esau when it's really a change of heart—from that of a liar and supplanter to that of a favorable man with God (as seen in the new name of the next verse).[129]

Isn't this questioning exactly what Jesus did for Peter on that beach in John 21? Perhaps, Peter is thinking about his denials and the, humanly speaking, role he had in the death of His friend Jesus. He's asked questions again to provoke a different outcome.

28 And He said, "Your name shall no longer be called Jacob, but [9]Israel; for you have struggled with God and with men, and have prevailed." Beginning with Esau during their births (Genesis 25).

29 Then Jacob asked, saying, "Tell me Your name, I pray." Exodus 6:1-3 tells us that the **name** of "God" was not known until Moses. So if it is the proper name of Creator God that Jacob was seeking, he's not going to get it. Exodus 6 tells us his **name** "Jehovah" was not revealed to anybody before Moses.

30 So Jacob called the name of the place [1]Peniel: "For I have

---

[129]The clarity of this statement is in thanks to my fellow pastor at Sandy Ridge Baptist Church, Zach Smith.

[9] Lit. *Prince with God*

seen God face to face, Here is the 2nd hint that Jacob knew he was wrestling a heavenly agent. This has much in common with the naming of the well by Hagar in Genesis 16. They named an occurrence with the angel of the LORD after God.

31 Just as he crossed over ²Penuel So he crossed another river or stream or brook. Why are these two different spellings? Perhaps one was the spelling at the time of the occurrence and the other was the spelling at the time of Moses' recording. Here is a great picture, by the way, of conversion. Before he **crossed over**, his name was changed. In both cases ("Jacob" and Israel") he is named after things he actually does/has.

32:31b-32

the sun rose on him, and he limped on his hip. We find no proof from Scripture that he was ever healed from his limping. The next verse shows perpetual testimony that many knew him as the limping man for the rest of his life. Do the math, and you will find that he wrestles with God at about 97 years old. He lives another 50 years with a limp. **32 Therefore to this day the children of Israel do not eat the muscle that shrank, which is on the hip socket, because He touched the socket of Jacob's hip in the muscle that shrank.** This is, by the way, a solid proof that if the angel wanted to hurt Jacob, he could've done so. He didn't need to wrestle with Jacob.

---

¹ Lit. *Face of God*
² Lit. *Face of God;* same as *Peniel,* v. 30

Chapter 33

33:4

But Esau ran to meet him, and embraced him, and fell on his neck and kissed him, and they wept. The last time Esau weeps is when Jacob rips off his blessings. Here, it is following Jacob's weeping and begging for a blessing from this angel (32:26). God, furthermore, is mending a relationship over which Jacob has no control.

33:17

It appears that Jacob lied to Esau again. He never does arrive, according to the biblical record, in Seir. Not only that, but he wasn't allowed to go there, it doesn't seem (31:13). Not only that, but he deliberately slowed the migration—apparently to buy time (33:14). Also, he resists the escort from Esau (33:15). On top of that we find out that Jacob goes to Succoth (first and only mention in Genesis) and then Shechem.

Chapter 34[130]

5 And Jacob heard that he had defiled Dinah his daughter. Now his sons were with his livestock in the field; so Jacob held his peace until they came. What is he thinking? How did he keep his peace?

7 And the sons of Jacob came in from the field when they heard it; and the men were grieved and very angry, because he had done a disgraceful thing in Israel. There was no patch of land known as "Israel." This is probably another pro-leptic speech. It is called that by the author before it was called that in actual, real time. This is evidence that somebody post-Moses added this pro-leptic title as Moses died before there was an "Israel." This land is not theirs yet (verse 1, 10-11), so it is not acceptable to say that some part of that land was "Israel." It should ultimately be noted that this is a moderator's comment. The sons of Jacob were upset that this was taking place in the land that was promised to them. "You are going to rape our sister in our own land?!" On the other hand, Exodus 9:7 helps us see that this could simply be shorthand for "in and among the people of Israel/Jacob." In either case, neither they nor their land was then called "Israel" so in both cases, it is a label given by the writer rather that than that which was attached at that time.

9 And make marriages with us; give your daughters to us, and take our daughters to yourselves. Probably, Jacob had more than one daughter. This was often summarized in Genesis 5 as "they had sons and daughters." With the age of only one woman in the whole Bible (Sarah), understating the number of women being born should be no surprise.

---

[130]See 38:1-5 also.
[131]See also under 2:1-3.

34:12

Ask me ever so much dowry and gift, Basically he's saying "name your price."

34:13-14

But the sons of Jacob answered Shechem and Hamor his father, and spoke deceitfully, because he had defiled Dinah their sister. The word in verse 2 is a different Hebrew word. This word is mostly a sexual reference to "deflowering." **14 And they said to them, "We cannot do this thing, to give our sister to one who is uncircumcised,** The only folks we know so far who in Genesis are practicing this are the Hebrews (or "sojourner").

34:17

But if you will not heed us and be circumcised, then we will take our daughter and be gone." This would have been a big deal with the economy if Jacob would pick up and leave town. There was probably a lot of trade already happening between these two peoples.

34:19-21

So the young man did not delay to do the thing, because he delighted in Jacob's daughter. There must be a level of expectation for **He was more honorable than all the household of his father.**

20 And Hamor and Shechem his son came to the gate of their city, and spoke with the men of their city, saying: We have also seen Lot at the gate of his city in Genesis 19 and when Abraham bargained with the men for the Cave of Macphelah in Genesis 23. **21 "These men are at peace with us. Therefore let them dwell**

159

in the land and trade in it. This is more than getting a daughter for Shechem. "This is good for your wallets." This was about a love of money again.

34:23

Will not their livestock, their property, and every animal of theirs be ours? Only let us consent to them, and they will dwell with us." They are both planning to deceive the other. Jacob's sons will prove to have hidden agenda while these men were about to make a trade agreement over the lust of the rich guy's son.

34:25

Now it came to pass on the third day, when they were in pain, How much pain? So much pain that they couldn't fight off two men.

34:29-30

and all their wealth. All their little ones and their wives they took captive; and they plundered even all that *was* in the houses. Think about the author being emphatic at this absolute slaughter. This is a sad day in Shechem. Multitudes of mothers and daughters are looking at their dead brothers and fathers and grandfathers. Now they're being taken from their homes. Taking in the entire scene…**30 Then Jacob said to Simeon and Levi,** Genesis 29:29-31 show these were the 2nd and 3rd sons of Jacob and Leah some twenty years ago (at least). You may remember Leah had six sons for her husband. This is all we see until here. We need to know that in this same passage of Genesis 30 we have Dinah being mentioned so that chapter 34 doesn't surprise us. **"You have troubled me by making me obnoxious among the inhabitants of the land, among the Canaanites and the Perizzites;** why talk about them? There are so many other nations mentioned in lists. Looking for these two as a pair in Genesis takes

160

us to only one other place. Genesis 12, 285 years previous to this episode (Abram was 75 in chapter 12; 100 when Isaac was born; Isaac was 60 when Jacob was born; Jacob is at least 100 years old in this story), speaks of Abraham returning from Egypt and finding strife with the herdsmen of the land. The lesson may very well be that Jacob was concerned about how these folks who knew his grandfather would think well of him. **and since I *am* few in number, they will gather themselves together against me and kill me. I shall be destroyed, my household and I.**" This seems rather under-scaled of a response to all these calamity by Jacob. He has a reason to be fearful, but these words don't grasp this gravity. Genesis 49 will show that he had a special disdain for this action of these two boys. It is on his mind in some of his last thoughts. He actually rebukes Reuben and then moves on to talk about the wrath of these two boys in 49:5-6 for their collapsing the walls of a whole city (moved around their defense). At the end of Genesis 47:28 we find that Jacob lived 147 years. If he was 97 when he left Laban then he has this on his mind for almost another half century! After all this, it seems odd that the priests would come from one of these angry boys (Levi).

Chapter 35

35:1

Then God said to Jacob, "Arise, go up in elevation (although "down" on a map) **to Bethel** where chapter 28's "ladder" episode took place.

35:2-4

And Jacob said to his ᵈhousehold and to all who *were* **with him,** The women from Shechem?

3 Then let us arise and go up to Bethel; and I will make an altar there to God, in addition to the one built in chapter 28 more than 30 years before.¹³² **who answered me in the day of my distress** trouble with Esau and Laban and the men of Shechem, etc…

4 So they gave Jacob all the foreign gods which *were* **in their hands,** which his favorite wife stole from her father (see chapter 31) or those they had gotten from Shechem (chapter 34).

35:6-7

So Jacob came to ˡLuz (that *is,* **Bethel),** The first of several geographical clarifications from the writer's perspective [in this chapter, verses 19 and 27 also)].

7 And he built an altar there perhaps 30 years before he had already built **an altar.**

ᵈGen. 18:19

¹³²This assumes Joseph was born around Jacob's 14ᵗʰ year with Laban (Genesis 30:25-26) and seeing Joseph's 18ᵗʰ year in Genesis 37. This leaves approximately 10-11 years between Joseph's birth and the episode of his being sold into slavery (Genesis 37).

ˡGen. 28:19, 22; 48:3

and called the place [2]**El Bethel,** It's more than just a place to him as He has met this God after Whom this place was named.

35:8

Now [o]**Deborah, Rebekah's nurse, died,** at more than 100 years old.[133] 27:42-45 seems to tell us how she may have come to Jacob in the first place. It could be, after 20 years with Laban, that it was time to return (of course, Jacob said it was a dream when explaining it to Laban, but it could have been both).

35:10-15

And God said to him, "Your name *is* **Jacob; your name shall not be called Jacob anymore, but Israel shall be your name." So He called his name Israel.** As discussed below, we surmise that this is not a 2nd renaming, but rather a review of the one renaming.

So just as we have an accounting of Jacob's renaming from Genesis 32, we have an accounting of the meeting of Bethel from Genesis 28. We seem to have an interweaving of these two chapters taking place here. It seems, rather than a reoccurrence of things that have already taken place, that this body of Scripture is a summary[134] of Jacob's journey "to this point." There are those who believe that this was an addition by a later editor,[135] and I am not

---

[2]Lit. *God of the House of God*

[o]Gen. 24:59

[133]Isaac, Genesis 24:59, Rebekah and her nurse went back to Isaac in his 40th year. 20 years later, Jacob and Esau were born. How many more years have passed? Well, we say that Joseph was born when Jacob was 91 years old, and Joseph is probably 6 or 7 now. That makes 118 years since the marriage of his father to his mother. Supposing that Deborah was 13 years old when she moved to be with Isaac, Deborah was 130 years old when she died.

[134]It could be that it was provided because it was a temporary ending to the book of Moses by Moses.

opposed to the idea. Remember what we have said: a general ascribing of the material to a single person allows for editors if there is a minor amount of changes.

> **Genesis 35:9 And God appeared unto Jacob again, when he came out of Padanaram, and blessed him** (Genesis 32:29). **10 And God said unto him, Thy name is Jacob: thy name shall not be called any more Jacob, but Israel shall be thy name: and he called his name Israel** (Genesis 32:28). **...12 And the land which I gave Abraham and Isaac, to thee I will give it, and to thy seed after thee will I give the land** (Genesis 28:13). **...14 And Jacob set up a pillar in the place where he talked with him, even a pillar of stone: and he poured a drink offering thereon, and he poured oil thereon** (Genesis 28:18). **15 And Jacob called the name of the place where God spake with him, Bethel** (Genesis 28:19).

35:18-20

And so it was, as her soul Used also in 1:20-21 to describe animals. So to say "animals don't go to Heaven because they don't have a **soul.** Don't forget that fish and birds have them too. 1:24 also uses this same Hebrew word for land animals. So we need to be careful when we say things like "animals don't have **souls.**" Scripture says they do! Now, we might say that a human **soul** is different from another **soul** might be true, but let's be precise if we can.

was departing after 25 years of marriage (13 with Laban and 10-11 since then).

---

[135]Herbert E. Ryle, The Book of Genesis in the Revised Version with Introduction and Notes, The Cambridge Bible for Schools and Colleges (Cambridge: Cambridge University Press, 1921), 338-339.

(for she died), This seems to be a Biblical definition of "death" (like James 2:26). **that she called his name [5]Ben-Oni; but his father called him [6]Benjamin. Ben,** clearly, means "son." Jesus, by the way, is God's **Ben-Oni** and **Benjamin** to us.

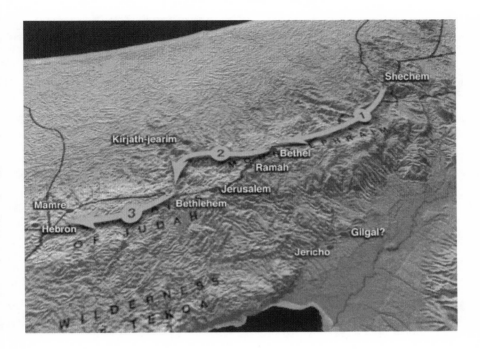

20 And Jacob set a pillar on her grave, which *is* the pillar of Rachel's grave to this day. The first one was erected at Bethel (Genesis 28) while the 2nd one was erected between Jacob and Laban (Genesis 31). This, then, is the 3rd **pillar** erected by Jacob. From the author's perspective, we see that, supposing it is Moses in this line, the spies of Numbers 13-14 told Moses about **Rachel's grave** from their tour of the Promised Land. We say this because Moses did not enter the Promised Land.

---

[5]Lit. *Son of My Sorrow*
[6]Lit. *Son of the Right Hand*

165

35:28-29

Now the days of Isaac were one hundred and eighty years.
Through simple math, using explicit statements of Jacob's age
when he entered Egypt—being 60 **years** younger than his dad—we
see that **Isaac** died 10 **years** before Jacob left Canaan for Egypt.
This also means, since we assume that the "two year mark into
famine" (Genesis 45) in Joseph's 40th year immediately preceded
Jacob's journey into Egypt, **Isaac** died without knowing the state
of Joseph. This is furthermore proof that these chapters are not
written in order. **29 So Isaac breathed his last and died, and was
gathered to his people, *being* old and full of days. And his sons
Esau and Jacob buried him.** Knowing the storyline of God, it
seems like I would then write about Judah because Jesus comes
from his line. But, other than the genealogy of Esau, the next
person we focus on is Joseph.

It looks as though the main character died and the story is over.
More proof, given the genealogy of the next chapter, that this book
was written in stages. Once Genesis 37 begins, **Isaac** doesn't
actually die for 12 more years. I wonder how that affected him.

Moreover, this verse and the next chapter conclude the
biographical information on **Esau.**

Chapter 36

36:1

Now this *is* the genealogy of Esau, who is Edom. Verses 8, 19, & 43 also say this to remind you that this is about Jacob's brother's people and perhaps to remind us how **Esau** got this name (Genesis 25:30).

36:3

Then I want you to notice all the possible connections between this genealogy and the book of Job. **Bashemath Ishmael's daughter, sister of Nebajoth** See verse 10 for more.

36:6-8

Then Esau took his wives, his sons, his daughters, and all the persons of his household, his cattle and all his animals, and all his goods which he had gained in the land of Canaan, and went to a country away from the presence of his brother Jacob. This is an apparent meeting in **Canaan** not discussed in Genesis. How do I know that? Because **Jacob** left before Esau in Genesis 27-28. It's nice to learn other items from the narrative in the middle of the genealogy. **7 For their possessions were too great for them to dwell together,** This sounds a lot like Genesis 13 (Abraham/Lot).

8 So Esau dwelt in Mount Seir. ʲEsau *is* Edom. It seems like 37:1 is in answer to this…thus making verses 9-43 were either parenthetical from the original author or was added by another author, or authors (people could have added to these genealogies much like generations of folks who hand their family Bible with the family section down to their children).

36:10

ʲGen. 36:1, 19

These are the names of Esau's sons; Eliphaz the son of Adah the wife of Esau. Eliphaz Esau's firstborn son. Eliphaz, in the book of Job, is one of the three friends of Job (Job 2). So **Eliphaz** is one of the three friends of Job. **Eliphaz,** Zophar, and Bildad are the three guys that show up to comfort Job and to some degree they were a comfort. But anyway, that's one connection. Another connection is probably in verse 33, "Bela died, and Jobab the son of Zerah of Bozrah reigned in his stead. And Jobab died." A lot of people think, I'm one of them, that's Job. The second king of Edom is a guy by the name of Jobab. Not to mention 36:28 features this guy in this genealogy several generations back named "Uz." Where is Job from? He lives in the land of Uz. Uz is in Edom. How do I know it's in Edom? I use a concordance and I find all the places where Uz is used and in Lamentations 4 it says that Uz is in Edom.

36:17

these are the sons of Reuel Esau's son; duke Nahath, duke Zerah, duke Shammah, duke Mizzah: these are the dukes that came of Reuel in the land of Edom. So we have **Reuel,** being in the land of Edom. **Reuel** and Jethro are names of Moses' father in law. He gave very good wisdom or advice to Moses in the time of him leading (Exodus 18) so there is definitely God's teaching going on in other strings of the descendants of Abraham other than just through the line of Isaac. God did not leave everyone else in the dark. No, he didn't. You have Job, and he knows something about a resurrection and a last day (Job 19:25).

36:28[136]

36:32

---

[136]See also 36:10.

And Bela the son of Beor reigned in Edom: and the name of his city was Dinhabah. We don't know exactly how many years past Moses this genealogy reaches, okay? It could go possibly many years past the writer, Moses, and again, that should tell you that Moses didn't write the entire genealogy. So if that's true, then, then this **Beor** should remind you of another character that's going to come along in Numbers: Balaam, son of **Beor**. So we could be very well dealing here with the brother of Balaam, the Moabite prophet in Numbers 24. So a lot of these people are found throughout the other parts of Scripture and that might be why their part of the genealogy was added.

36:33[137]

Reuel is another name for Moses' father-in-law. I'm just trying to get you to see that there is a lot of stuff buried in these genealogies if you care enough to read them.

36:35

And Husham died, and Hadad the son of Bedad, who smote Midian a son of Abraham's through his 2nd wife Keturah (25:1-2). **in the field of Moab** So here is this Midian character and we find out when he died it was in chapter 36. So now you are getting an idea that some of these people that are related to Esau are killing fellow kinsmen, right? **reigned in his stead: and the name of his city was Avith.**
Now how is Esau related to Abraham? Esau is a grandson of Abraham. What would **Midian** be to Esau? An uncle. Esau's father is Isaac and Abraham is Isaac's father and **Midian**'s father, right? So that would make **Midian** an uncle to Esau. So Esau's people are at least involved with killing the people of his uncle.

These places are named that because later on their descendants

---

[137]See also 36:10.

gave them, or I should say they took on the name of the people that settled there. So Edom, **Moab**, Ammon, **Midian** all here southeast of the Dead Sea in what you might call the Jordan Valley.

36:12-14

Now Timna was the concubine of Eliphaz, Esau's son, Is this one of Job's friends (Job 2)? We would quickly say no if it were not for the fact that a king named "Jobab" also appears in this passage. **and she bore Amalek** 14:7 first mentions the **Amalek**ites in the lifetime of Abraham. It must be, then, that this is the 2nd **Amalek** in the Scripture.

14 These were the sons of [4]Aholibamah, Esau's wife, the daughter of Anah, the daughter of Zibeon. And she bore to Esau: Jeush, Jaalam, and Korah. Almost entirely repeated in verses 15-18. The only addition is the word "chief" in those verses.

36:20-21

These *were* the sons of Seir the Horite Esau married into them (his firstborn son does, rather). That's how these next 11 verses got in here.

21 Dishon, Ezer, and Dishan. These *were* the chiefs of the Horites, the sons of Seir, in the land of Edom. Verses 20-21 are almost identical to verses 29-30 other than the addition, again, of "duke/chief".

36:31

Now these *were* the kings who reigned in the land of Edom before any king reigned over the children of Israel: Probably

---

[4]Or *Oholibamah*

added after Moses since it's written from a perspective in which there was a **king over Israel.**[138]

---

[138]See under introduction.

Chapter 37

37:1-2

Now Jacob dwelt in the land This was probably a contrasting statement with the place where the other line was living (36:8).

2 This *is* the history of Jacob. Joseph, *being* seventeen years old, This is one of the figures we use to determine how old Jacob was at the time of his fleeing into Haran (by subtracting this from Joseph's age given in 41:36). These, in turn, are used to give us [assuming a 966 B.C. building of Solomon's temple (1 Kings 6:1) to start the count backwards (using Exodus 12:40 and Galatians 3:17 to get the clock started forward in Abram's 76th year)]. **was feeding the flock with his brothers. And the lad *was* with the sons of Bilhah and the sons of Zilpah,** where are Leah's **sons** (Rachel's other son was Benjamin and too young to be away from dad)? I am not sure if it was just a point of record or not, but it seems like we shouldn't assume any information is mere "by the way" in God's Word.

his father's wives; So we see how handmaidens were counted—assuming there wasn't a change in status since they were given to he and his wives by Laban.

37:3

Now Israel loved Joseph more where did he learn to show more **love** to one son more than the other? His parents (Genesis 26-27). **than all his children, because he *was* the son of his old age.** 44:20 uses this same description about Benjamin.[139]

37:6

---

[139]First pointed out to me by our friend Jamie Styles, teacher at BBA and a member of my SS class at BBC.

So he said to them, "Please hear this dream which I have dreamed: while no overt sin is assigned to **Joseph** in the Scripture, one might question his wisdom.

37:9

Then he dreamed still another dream It seems as though we are having the same dream twice. Why? 41:32 teaches us that two **dream**s of quick succession mean a soon fulfillment. 41:46 tell us that it has been 13 years since the **dream** (with 37:2). 46:2 tells us he is 39 years old (being 9 years through the afore-promised 14 years of dreams in chapter 41), and it has been 22 years since "quick" was promised to Joseph. But wait…God has been working moving pieces preparing for the fulfillment.

and told it to his brothers, and said, "Look, I have dreamed another dream. And this time, gthe sun, the moon, and the eleven stars assuming we are not making reference to Diana, we have to assume that Joseph is born (we thought so anyway since mother died giving birth to him in chapter 35).

37:11

And his brothers envied him, but his father kept the matter *in mind*. See Genesis 42:6-9, 43:26, 44:14, and 50:18 for this dream fulfilled.

37:17

And the man said, "They have departed from here, for I heard them say, 'Let us go to Dothan.' " So Joseph went after his brothers and found them in ⁿDothan.[140] 13 or more miles from

---

gGen. 46:29; 47:25

n2 Kin. 6:13

[140]See map. I don't know the source of the map and will update future versions of this book as the source comes to light.

where he was expecting to find them.

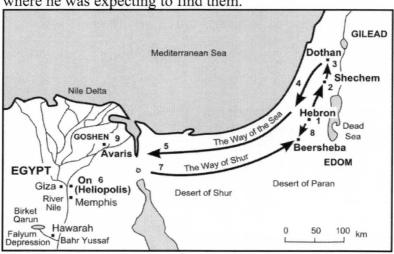

37:25

And they sat down to eat a meal. Then they lifted their eyes and looked, and there was a company of ᵗIshmaelites, These were not supposed to happen…yet Abraham's sin worked out for the saving of many (50:20) in Joseph, and the saving of the world through Judah (Revelation 5:5). If Joseph is not sold into slavery through this "unplanned" pregnancy (from our perspective), then Jacob's family dies in the famine of Canaan and Israel as a nation stops, Genesis 3:15, and Genesis 12:3 don't occur, and we all die in our sins.

ᵗGen. 16:11, 12; 37:28, 36; 39:1

174

Chapter 38

38:1-5[141]

It came to pass at that time It would be interesting to know what drove him away **from his brothers, and visited** It could be, then, that this was during their time in Shechem or shortly thereafter, but the natural reading here—and the placement of these episodes— seems to place this on the heels of what happened to Joseph in chapter 37.

2 And Judah saw there a daughter of a certain Canaanite whose name *was* Shua, and he married her and went in to her. For the 2nd of 3 times, then, we shall have a chapter centered, in part, around a woman (see chapters 34 and 39). **3 So she conceived and bore a son,** so nearly a year has passed.

4 She conceived again So it is probable that we have another year passing.

5 And she conceived yet again and bore a son, and called his name Shelah. So if she has had a few months' rest, a total of three years has passed. Joseph, 37:2, is probably in Potiphar's prison. **He was at Chezib** apparently the same as "Achzib."[142]

38:6-10[143]

Then Judah took a wife for Er his firstborn, How old was this oldest son? He was old enough to procreate and be a husband, but if the chronology of Joseph's life is accurate (and it is); and Joseph is 13 years older when he stand before Pharaoah, and the brothers

---

[141]See also 2:1-3 & 39:12-16.

[142] Walter A. Elwell and Barry J. Beitzel, "Achzib," *Baker Encyclopedia of the Bible* (Grand Rapids, MI: Baker Book House, 1988), 17.

[143]See under 22:8 as well.

come in Joseph's 37th year (after the famine begun), then this episode probably took place in the 20 years between Joseph's sale into Egypt (last chapter) and the first trip to Egypt (chapter 42) from **Judah** and the other 9 brothers who went. **and her name *was* Tamar.** Not the daughter of David (2 Samuel 13).

7 But Er, Judah's firstborn, was wicked in the sight of the LORD, ʲand the LORD killed him. Moses doesn't mind interpreting history without even providing the actual narrative of how **Er** was **killed.** If he was old enough to be married and put to death by God, then we are nearly famine time, but then the following occurs:

9 But Onan knew that the heir would not be his; and it came to pass, when he went in to his brother's wife, that he emitted on the ground Here's a great opportunity to discuss birth control. It seems at the outset that this is a strong case against birth control and self-gratification, but these seem a little outside the intended context of a man breaking the pre-law law.[144] **lest he should give**

ʲ1 Chr. 2:3

[144]Let us consider what the Roman Catholic Church teaches its youth: _____*Youth Catechism of the Catholic Church* (San Francisco: Ignatius Press, 2010), 229; **Er** and **Onan** provide for us a discussion concerning birth control and the Roman Catholic Church.
From the Youth Catechism:

"Why are all methods of preventing the conception of a child not equally good?"

The Church recommends the refined methods of self-observation and natural family planning as methods of deliberately regulating conception.

Alright here's, again their words, but first they quote from Pope John Paul II who says,

When couples (have) recourse to contraception…they manipulate and degrade human sexuality—and with it themselves and their married

an heir to his brother. Was it because he hated **his brother** and wanted nothing to bring him legacy? Was it because he didn't want to provide for this new family? **10 And the thing which he did displeased the LORD; therefore He killed him also.** Again, no explanation by Moses the author. For two sons to fail at marriage we are almost certainly toward the passing of the afore-mentioned 20 years.

---

partner—by altering its value of total self-giving.

What do they mean? Pope John Paul II appears to be saying that the full value of marital relationship is found in sexual relationship that results in the possibility of having children and that if you want to commit yourself to your spouse, then you do so without contraception. You give of yourself by allowing for the production of children and if you are doing anything to alter that process, you're actually not giving of yourself to your spouse because you are inhibiting the natural process.

So the RCC thinks that you should not be indifferent about whether or not you manipulate your fertility, ladies, or manipulate the fertility of your wife, men.

> Natural Family Planning is called natural: it is ecological, holistic, healthy, and an exercise in partnership. On the other hand, the Church rejects all artificial means of contraception. The Church rejects all artificial means of contraception—namely, chemical methods (the 'Pill'), mechanical methods (for example, condom, intra-uterine device, or IUD), and surgical methods (sterilization)—since these attempt to separate the sexual act from its procreative potential and block the total self-giving of husband and wife.

Now think about this, think about all the Catholics you know and ask yourself, do they believe this? Then you can actually start a conversation by saying, "Are you a good Catholic? Think about what the pope says or the Church says about…" This is intended for the youth and this was published in 2010. So this is not, "Oh, they taught that, they don't believe that anymore." Yes, they do.

Genesis 38 may not mean what the RCC says it means but you have to settle this in your mind as Bible-believers: It don't mean nothing. Alright, so if it doesn't mean what they say it means, you have to decide what it means because it means something. So you have to be honest enough with yourself to say, "Okay, this is not God frowning on birth control." Alright then, what does it mean? You have to decide it means something and if you're willing to take the risk of upsetting the Lord by sinning against Him.

38:11

Then Judah said to Tamar his daughter-in-law, [n]"Remain a widow in your father's house till my son Shelah is grown." For he said, "Lest he also die like his brothers." Maybe **Judah** was suspicious of Tamar's part in his sons' deaths, or maybe **Judah** was really concerned that he would be completely bereft of his sons if **Shelah** wasn't given the chance to make this right. It's hard to believe that this young man would have been growing up knowing to whom he was already supposed to be married.

38:12-16

Now in the process of time the daughter of Shua, Judah's wife, died He is sad after having lost his two sons and now his **wife** (found in 38:2). **and Judah was comforted, and went up to his sheepshearers at Timnah, he and his friend Hirah the Adullamite.** Whom he had visited nearly 20 years before (verse 1).

14 So she took off her widow's garments So just as we discovered that there were wedding garments (Genesis 29) and **widow's garments** (see also 38:19), we will soon find that there are such things as the **garments** of a harlot (see verse 15 and compare with Proverbs 7:10). **covered** *herself* **with a veil and wrapped herself, and sat in an open place which** *was* **on the way to Timnah** it should interest the Bible reader that Judges 14:1 shows us this is where Samson got his trouble-girl. One would wonder if this parallel, along with Genesis 19/Judges 19:22 are meant to instruct us of other Genesis/Judges parallels. Of course, considering the Genesis 19 connection below, one only feels vindicated to seeing these themes.

---

[n]Ruth 1:12, 13

16 Then he turned to her by the way, and said, "Please let me come in to you" what a strange book. We could say that between Noah's drunkenness (chapter 9) and Lot's drunkenness (chapter 19) we could very well have another case of "rebound sex" (even with close relations) for those who are just on the downside of things. Life lesson: we tend to say and do things when we are sad or drunk we would not normally do.

38:24

And it came to pass, about three months after, that Judah was told, saying, "Tamar your daughter-in-law has played the harlot; furthermore she *is* with child by harlotry." So Judah said, "Bring her out and let her be burned!" Another hint of pre-Mosaic law:[145] The daughters of priests were to be **burned** (Leviticus 21:9) but the general practice was stoning (Deuteronomy 22:21) so, as hard as it seems to be to believe, the Mosaic law was a bit more merciful.

38:26

So Judah acknowledged *them* and said, "She has been more righteous than I, because I did not give her to Shelah my son." And It makes a person wonder if **Judah** was embarrassed most at his lack of integrity with **Shelah** being given to another woman or his own lack of temperance regarding his relationship with a supposed harlot, but **he never knew her again.** Along with the other strange practices in this book are the realities that it seems as though **Judah** did not act as a husband [which would have entitled Tamar to be free from him under Moses (Exodus 21:7-11)]. It seems as though he did father the boys that are to be born though (46:8-12).

---

[145]Besides levirate marriage and clean animals with Noah and laws for sacrifice (4:4).

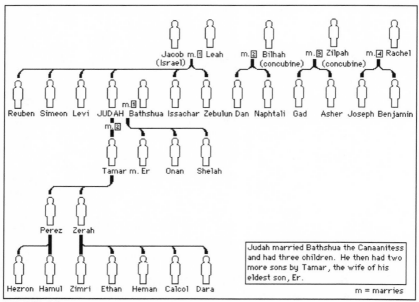

Judah married Bathshua the Canaanitess and had three children. He then had two more sons by Tamar, the wife of his eldest son, Er.

m = marries

38:27-30

Now it came to pass, at the time for giving birth, that behold, twins *were* in her womb. Here we are again, twins 2.0 (see chapter 25).

29 Then it happened, as he drew back his hand, that his brother came out unexpectedly; and she said, "How did you break through? *This* breach *be* upon you!" Therefore his name was called Perez.[4] and he became the great ancestor of Jesus Christ (twice over if you see both Matthew 1 and Luke 3). See chart to the right.[146]

---

[4]Lit. *Breach* or *Breakthrough*

[146] H. L. Ellison, "Judah," ed. D. R. W. Wood et al., *New Bible Dictionary* (Leicester, England; Downers Grove, IL: InterVarsity Press, 1996), 621.

Chapter 39

Once again, after chapter 34 with Dinah and chapter 38 with Tamar, we have another chapter where a sexual scandal is the main event of the chapter.

39:1-3

Now Joseph had been taken down to Egypt. And Potiphar, an officer In some versions this could be translated "eunuch." One would wonder if this is why his wife later has sexual interest in Joseph. **of Pharaoh, captain of the guard, an Egyptian, bought him from the Ishmaelites** Humanly speaking, they should not have existed. This was Abraham's foul. Somehow, now, Ishmael is numerous in his descendants.

3 And his master saw that the LORD was with him and that the LORD made all he did to prosper in his hand. This is why Joseph is ultimately trusted with the estate of Potiphar.

39:5

So it was, from the time that he had made him overseer of his house and all that he had, that the LORD blessed the Egyptian's house for Joseph's sake; Genesis 31 finds Jacob being a blessing to the household of Laban simply because the Lord was with him. This is a pattern, to say the least, of God blessing those around His people for the sake of His people. Also, Genesis 20 and Genesis 26 find Abimelech being blessed because of the presence of Abraham and Isaac. These are lessons that God blesses us despite the wicked, and then sometimes blesses the wicked because of us. Sometimes the reason He keeps us in certain places at the cost of our comfort is so that He can save others from certain calamity. **and the blessing of the LORD was on all that he had in the house and in the field.** God still blesses countries when His people are present. Nothing has changed since God is still God.[147]

39:6-9

Thus he left all that he had in Joseph's hand, and he did not know what he had except for the bread which he ate. "It's all in hand with you. Call me for lunch. I'll be golfing." He trusted Joseph.

Now Joseph was handsome in form and appearance. This is the first time a male's appearance is mentioned, and it "just so happens" that this is the way his mother Rachel is described in Genesis 29:17. **7 And it came to pass after these things that his master's wife cast longing eyes on Joseph, and she said, "Lie with me."** Apparently, ladies can be attracted to men's appearance. So much for the so-called notion that they are not interested in sex and are just turned on emotionally. If it's true at all, this woman was unusual. God gave both Adam and Eve coats of skin. It's not just women who should be modest. Women can be enticed as well.

8 But he refused and said to his master's wife, "Look, my master does not know what is with me in the house, and he has committed all that he has to my hand. Joseph felt the weight of being trusted so heavily. **9 There is no one greater in this house than I,** Potiphar trusted Joseph even more than his own wife. This is an interesting piece of information when one considers whether this was a virtuous woman or not. **nor has he kept back anything from me but you, because you are his wife. How then can I do this great wickedness, and sin against God?"** This was not a sin against Potiphar primarily. It was a sin against God. This is quite a well-developed understanding of sin which may be a reflection of his sense of God's presence in his life earlier in this chapter. The biggest issue for Joseph was that he was upsetting the Lord. This is

---

[147]https://www.christianpost.com/news/david-cameron-says-britain-must-stand-up-against-global-christian-persecution-urges-increased-evangelism-117845/ [accessed 12/5/2018].

why we have a world full of people who have not made the connection between their conduct and their destiny.

39:11-16

But it happened about this time, when Joseph went into the house to do his work, and none of the men of the house was inside, We will not implicate Joseph. It is a huge building, no doubt, and he has little or no knowledge of who is behind every turn or in every room. **12 that she caught him by his garment, saying, "Lie with me." But he left his garment in her hand, and fled and ran outside.** This is the 2nd time Joseph lost his coat. Folks can take anything from you, but they don't have to take your identity. They can you're your coat, but you have to surrender your character. You don't have to change just because people hope to change you.

14 that she called to the men of her house and spoke to them, saying, "See, he has brought in to us a Hebrew to mock us. He came in to me to lie with me, and I cried out with a loud voice. She goes from lying about Joseph to slandering her husband's judgment.

16 So she kept his garment with her until his master came home. She had a lot of time to do this and that being in a pampered, powerful position. Ezekiel 16:47-48 tell us that Sodom's sexual sin was a result of their idleness, in part. She had time to offer daily propositions to Joseph?

39:20-21

Then Joseph's master took him and put him into the prison, a place where the king's prisoners were confined. And he was there in the prison. This could be just "saving face." I mean, what do you do if your woman is running around after a servant? So even if he knew his wife's character....he couldn't let her take the fall. Think about Vashti, the king at the beginning of Esther. The reason she was disposed of had nothing to do with her transgression as much as news getting around that the queen was getting away with being insubordinate. The idea was that other wives would find out and do the same thing to their husbands. **21 But the LORD was with Joseph** even in prison. He isn't alone.

39:22-23

And the keeper of the prison committed to Joseph's hand all the prisoners who were in the prison; whatever they did there, it was his doing. 2nd time, same chapter. **23 The keeper of the prison did not look into anything that was under Joseph's authority,** He and Potiphar are playing golf and wondering how they both had this handy fellow in their jurisdiction. Perhaps the jailer knew the story about Joseph in Potiphar's home and maybe Potiphar knew Joseph was in that particular jail. Perhaps they didn't spend time around each other either.

Chapter 40

There are no notes for this chapter.

Chapter 41

41:1[148]

Then it came to pass, at the end of two full years, Well, it seems as though the butler forgot about Joseph, but let's see if God has. We're going to find out that Joseph is nearly 30 years old which means it has been 13 years since he left home, and if he spent a year in Potiphar's house (I don't know how long it was), then he has been in jail 12 years.

For what?!

For Him to learn the interpretation of **dream**s and to await the situation which requires his presence before **Pharaoh** who **had a dream; and behold, he stood by the river.** Probably the Nile.

41:9-12

Then the chief butler or "cup-bearer" as he "pressed into the cup" or tested wine **spoke to Pharaoh, saying: "I remember my faults this day.** "Oh boy...what have I done?" So after saying "I've got you covered" to Joseph, he forgot. The book of Jasher says this took place as punishment from God for Joseph's trusting the butler in lieu of him. In any case, though, God was not late. It was uncomfortable, doubtless, for Joseph...but God was not aloof from the redeeming value behind Joseph's condition. The **butler**'s forgetfulness needed to happen long enough for **Pharaoh** to dream! **10 When Pharaoh was angry with his servants,** Perhaps this is a different **Pharaoh** since this man has to remind him of what he did?

12 Now there was a young Hebrew a "stateless" man or a wanderer. **man with us there, a servant of the captain of the guard.**

---

[148]See also under 41:17-24 for 41:2-8.

41:13

And it came to pass, just ᵐas he interpreted for us, so it
happened. He restored me to my office, and he hanged him."
What we just saw in these verses is a summary of chapter 40.

41:14-15

ⁿThen Pharaoh sent and called Joseph, and they ᵒbrought him
quickly ᵖout of the dungeon; and he shaved, changed his
clothing, apparently people have sense to dress and groom in
specific ways when approaching rulers.

15 And Pharaoh said to Joseph, "I have had a dream, and *there
is* no one who can interpret it. ʳBut I have heard it said of you
that you can understand a dream, to interpret it." Apparently
the idea of "I don't care what people think about me" doesn't work
well when people are speaking of your credentials. If **Joseph**
returns evil for evil with the butler, there is a chance the butler will
not tell **Pharaoh** of this man back in prison.

41:17-24

These verses are a replay of verses 2-8 from the mouth of
Pharaoh.

41:25

ᵐGen. 40:21, 22
ⁿPs. 105:20
ᵒDan. 2:25
ᵖ1 Sam. 2:8
ʳGen. 41:8, 12; Dan. 5:16

Then Joseph said to Pharaoh, "The dreams of Pharaoh *are* one; This is the 3rd set of two dreams (after Joseph's in chapter 37 and the Butler/Baker set of two in Genesis 40).

41:29-32

Indeed seven years of great plenty will come throughout all the land of Egypt; apparently this is not a famine of all food in all places. Later in Genesis 43:11 there are some foods available in Canaan. To have cattle, for example, these nations would have needed some feed for those animals.

32 And the dream was repeated to Pharaoh twice because the thing is established by God, and God will shortly bring it to pass. Here we are again. Why two dreams in the same night? Because it will happen quickly. Apparently, this is why there were two dreams in Genesis 37 as well? It's hard to imagine that at this point, his brothers have not bowed to him; it has been 13 years, and yet, it was "quickly?"

41:34

Let Pharaoh do this, and let him appoint officers over the land, to collect one-fifth of the produce of the land of Egypt in the seven plentiful years. Unless you can find a better principle in the Proverbs or something, this is a great goal for everyone to save when things are good.

41:38

And Pharaoh said to his servants, "Can we find such a one as this, a man in whom is the Spirit of God?" Does Pharaoh have a good understanding of the 3rd person of the Trinity? Think he was reading systematic theology? Probably not.

In Genesis 1:2, we find "the Spirit of God" but, He is, of course, not called "the 3rd Person of the Trinity." The "Spirit of God" was present on the first day of Creation. Light occurs in 1:3, but the evening happens first. Genesis 3:8 speaks of the "spirit of the day" being that in which one may walk. So it can be a Person, yes. However, it can also be a simple "wind." The word in the Greek New Testament is *pneuma* and we often know of sicknesses and tools that have this word and we know that it deals with wind. Therefore, when we speak of the "Holy Spirit," we are talking about the "Holy Wind of God" or "Holy Breath of God." Here, Pharaoh could have been simply saying "Does anybody have the breath of God within them?"

Then there is Genesis 8:1. It is not translated "spirit" (Genesis 1:2) or "cool" (Genesis 3:8), but it is translated "wind." Translation committees know there are several possible translations for many words. We are only saying all this to say that Pharaoh may not be exactly asking for the 3rd Person of the Trinity. Every time we speak, we have a puff of air come from our mouths. Pharaoh could be simply asking "does anybody have the words of God like Joseph?"

41:45

And Pharaoh called Joseph's name Zaphnath-Paaneah. This name means "resting in the treasury" but in this context he is being called "savior of Egypt" or in the big picture "savior of the world." **And he gave him as a wife Asenath,** this name means "dedicated to Nath" which is an Egyptian goddess which is the equivalent to the Roman "Minerva."

41:46

Joseph was thirty years old when he stood before Pharaoh king of Egypt. For 13 years he has been gone. How did he learn how to interpret dreams? He has already once interpreted dreams to his brothers. Then, he did the same for two officers in the prison. Just because one may not be "doing much," that doesn't mean they are not accomplishing anything. There has also been some maturation. A 17-year old would probably tell a 2nd dream with a message already given in an angering first dream to his brothers. Some maturation was needed and these years probably provided it.

41:49

Joseph gathered very much grain, as the sand of the sea, until he stopped counting, for it was immeasurable. Many folks, on behalf of Joseph, are tallying the incoming produce. At some point, they all tossed their clipboards over their shoulders and quit counting.

Now, there's no question that Joseph is a great picture of Jesus. Now, consider that he is also a great picture of the antichrist—typically knowns as the "beast" in Revelation. Maybe a better way to say it is that the Antichrist—seeking to be a picture of Christ, is a twisted anti-type of Joseph (especially in view of Matthew 28:18 and the Christ who really does have all authority in heaven and earth). Revelation 13:1 speaks of this "beast." Revelation 13:4 says the "dragon gave him his power." The "whole world wondered after the beast who has this sway over the whole world, and he received worship. Pharaoh gave all power to Joseph and he receives adoration from all these from the known world who lean on him for sustenance as will be seen later in the next chapter. Interesting, at the end of Revelation 13 there is a desperation for food (in light of the four horsemen of Revelation 6) to the point where people are driven to take a "mark." The point is, one can see a foreshadowing of this conqueror who uses food to leverage his power and allegiance from the people. In other words, he controls the world through food in a scenario where—in the next chapter—we see money and riches does nothing for starving people.

God the Father and Jesus are the perfect fulfillment of Joseph and Pharaoh while the dragon and the beast are the imperfect or corrupt fulfillment of Joseph and Pharaoh.

41:51

And Joseph called the name of the firstborn Manasseh: For God, said he, hath made me forget all my toil, and all my father's house. So Manasseh means really "forgetting." **And the name of the second called he Ephraim: For God hath caused me to be fruitful in the land of my affliction.** So he looks at one son and he thinks about forgetting the old toil, and he looks at the other son and he thinks about fruitful land in the middle of his affliction.

I'm not going to be dogmatic here but it looks like these could be twins. They're at least a set. They're at least children that were born close enough to each other that we know that they were born definitely within seven years of each other because the famine hasn't started and it says that after he stood before Pharaoh at 30 he was given a wife, and before the years of famine she gave him two sons. I suppose they're as much twins as Cain and Abel and we don't know that they were twins but they were certainly born close, one after the other.

41:55

And when all the land of Egypt was famished, the people cried to Pharaoh for bread: and Pharaoh said unto all the Egyptians, Go unto Joseph; what he saith to you, do. Now this is kind of interesting if you think about it. There's a famine throughout the whole world except in this little place.

41:57

And all countries came into Egypt to Joseph for to buy corn; because that the famine was so sore in all lands. Now when Jacob saw that there was corn in Egypt, Jacob said unto his

sons, Why do ye look one upon another? Alright, now this is a little funny. For one thing, we need to remember there's not a total famine. Remember in chapter 43 we found out that they're actually taking things as presents to Joseph. They have some food but the grain, the bread, that kind of thing, there is none.

Joseph is now, since the famine has begun, 37. Now we know that because we're using simple stuff here: verse 46 says he was 30 when he stood before Pharaoh, seven years of plenteousness have passed, the famine is upon them, he's at least 37 years old. Now he was 17 when he was sold into slavery, 20 years have passed. Remember we've talked before about how Joseph was born probably 14 years into Jacob's stay with Laban, six years left there. Some of Joseph's older brothers are almost 7 years older than he is.[149]

So picture Jacob now. Jacob we're going to find out, dies at 147. He spent 17 of those years in Egypt. So Jacob, Joseph's dad, is 130 when he comes to Egypt. That's about seven years away at this point. So he's about 120 years old looking at a bunch of guys in their younger 30s saying, "Why are y'all looking at each other?" Now these men have families. If you're not sure of that, review chapter 38 where Judah is old enough to have married off a third and quite younger son, Shelah, to this daughter-in-law Tamar, remember? So they all have families and dad doesn't mind invoking the right of patriarchy to tell some boys to get off their...and move south and get some food.

When these brothers sold Joseph into slavery, you probably expected him to work himself to death very quickly. They even told Joseph that Joseph's dead. They assume he is. They didn't even sit around and think, "Joseph's made it." Not only is he in a different place but he's in a different position than they expect him to be. He shouldn't be alive, let alone, number 2 in the world. Now

---

[149]First of his brothers was born nearly 8 years after Jacob began working for Laban.

192

that's a corporate climb.

So there has been some maturing with Joseph. I do not want to paint this pristine picture that Joseph was just faultless. Now there's no recorded sins per se of him in Scripture but there's a fantastic difference between saying that someone is "sinless in Moses' account" and saying that they're sinless. It's a little different.

Chapter 42

42:1-3

When Jacob saw that there was grain in Egypt, Jacob said to his sons, "Why do you look at one another?" A man in excess of 100 years old is offering this fantastic sarcasm. **2 And he said, "Indeed I have heard** probably from people returning northward from there along the same trade routes upon which the Ishmaelites had been traveling southward in Genesis 37.

that there is grain in Egypt; of all places, he hears of help in the very place where his beloved son has been for the last 13-15 years (see this later).

3 And Joseph's ten brethren went down to buy corn in Egypt. Now how old is Benjamin about this time? Joseph was born six years before they left Laban's. So six years with Laban, 10 years in Shechem and in their sojourn from Shechem south is when Rachel died giving birth to Benjamin. So Benjamin is about 15-16 years younger than Joseph and so Benjamin is about 21-22 years old. So he's still not allowed to go because he is the remaining son from the favorite wife, okay, and he's the youngest, so who knows why he wasn't allowed to go but verse 4.

42:4

But Benjamin, Joseph's brother, Jacob sent not with his brethren; for he said, Lest peradventure mischief befall him. "Just in case. We've done this before."

42:6-7

Now Joseph *was* governor over the land; In effect, he was—both immediately (for the world that was then) and telescopically (in providing Jesus through Judah his brother)—the savior of the world. **and it was he who sold to all the people of the land. And**

194

Joseph's brothers came and ᶠbowed down before him with *their* faces to the earth. This is the fulfillment of **Joseph's** dreams in chapter 37. **7 Joseph saw his brothers** The oldest of which is no more than 7 years older if his father had no wife for 7 years (Genesis 29), then had two wives in a single week, and then all children minus Benjamin were born prior to the end of the 7 years Jacob worked for Rachel (Genesis 30). **and recognized them, but he acted as a stranger to them and spoke roughly to them.** We'll find out this was through an interpreter.

Do you remember that when Jesus got to the people's house in Emmaus? It says that Jesus made as though he would have gone on further. In other words, "I really don't have time to stay for supper." And remember they begged him to stay. "Oh, please stay with us!" Remember that? So great parallel.

42:10

And they said unto him, Nay, my lord, but to buy food are thy servants come. We are all one man's sons; we are true men, thy servants are no spies. And he said unto them, Nay, but to see the nakedness of the land ye are come. Now remember we'll find out later that Joseph is not speaking to them in their language. He's speaking to them through an interpreter so Joseph's a good role-player. How does he act like he's not understanding them when he totally understands them? He recognizes them, they don't recognize him. He is hearing what they're saying and they don't know that he's hearing what they're saying and you're going to find out later in the passage when they're telling on themselves, he hears it.

So think about two things. 1. This discussion is taking a long time to happen. "No, no, no, we're here, tell him we're here." And he says, "No, they're lying." And the interpreter says, "You're lying.

ᶠGen. 37:7–10; 41:43

195

You're here as spies." Now think about this. When we say Joseph is speaking Egyptian, you need to know that it's not Egyptian like today's Egyptian. For one thing, there was a dynasty change after Joseph, and that's why the writer of Exodus says there was a Pharaoh that did not know Joseph. Well, how is that possible? Well, there's a complete dynasty change.

Anyway, he knows the language of the people who are in charge in Egypt but did he know that going down into Egypt? As he's sold by the Midianites into the Egyptian's hand, all of a sudden you have Midianites maybe speaking Hebrew? Then they are speaking to the people they sold him to at Potiphar's house, right? And they're speaking in a language, and Joseph is not only in an Egyptian prison but he is actually learning the language of the Egyptians, enough that he can actually communicate with Pharaoh and then act in his stead like he belongs there. Then he's able to communicate with such fluency that his brothers don't even suspect anything.

42:13

And they said, Thy servants are twelve brethren, the sons of one man in the land of Canaan; and, behold, the youngest is this day with our father, and one is not. "He's dead. **And Joseph said unto them, That is it that I spake unto you, saying, Ye are spies.** So in case you missed the first three times, verse 9, verse 10 and verse 12, I'm going to say it again, **You're spies.**

42:15-17

Hereby ye shall be proved: By the life of Pharaoh ye shall not go forth hence, "By the life of Pharaoh ye shall not go forth hence except your youngest brother come hither." Now what does Joseph want? He wants to see his kid brother. He's not interested in vengeance. Maybe he is. I mean, he is making them sweat a little bit, isn't he? But he is most interested in seeing his brother that he

196

hasn't seen in 20 years.

16 Send one of you, and let him fetch your brother, and ye shall be kept in prison. I think it's interesting to note that it took 20 years for Joseph to see his dream fulfilled.

that your words may be proved, whether there be any truth in you: or else by the life of Pharaoh surely ye are spies. Number 5 time he says it.

17 And he put them all together into ward three days. This made a difference to **Joseph.**

And Joseph said unto them the third day, This do, and live; for I fear God. "I've changed my mind. Instead of sending one of you"…

42:19

If ye be true men, let one of your brethren be bound in the house of your prison: go ye, carry corn for the famine of your houses. Now who knows what Joseph is doing here but he has changed from, "I'm sending one and keeping 10," to "I'm keeping one and sending 10."

42:20

bring your youngest brother unto me; so shall your words be verified, and ye shall not die. So, "I will find you and kill you if I feel like you're lying to me." And you'd better know that the lord of the country had the resources to make a 200 mile trip and make it happen. "I'll hang you on posts around the city."

> *37:21 Reuben heard it, and he delivered him out of their hands; and said, Let us not kill him. And Reuben said unto them, Shed no blood, but cast him into this pit that is in the*

197

wilderness.

We have Reuben, verse 29, has gone somewhere and done something because he returns and Joseph is gone. Verse 26 places the scheming in Judah's lap. Maybe Simeon is kept behind here because as the 2nd oldest, he approved of Joseph's slavery sale in Reuben's absence?

> Numbers 26:1 And it came to pass after the plague, that the LORD spake unto Moses and unto Eleazar the son of Aaron the priest, saying, Take the sum of all the congregation of the children of Israel, from twenty years old and upward, throughout their fathers' house, all that are able to go to war in Israel.

"So let's count all the sword-swingers that we have here at our disposal and let's go by tribes."

> Verse 3, Moses and Eleazar the priest spake with them in the plains of Moab by Jordan near Jericho, saying, Take the sum of the people, from twenty years old and upward; as the LORD commanded Moses and the children of Israel, which went forth out of the land of Egypt.

> Verse 5 Reuben, the eldest son of Israel: the children of Reuben…7 These are the families of the Reubenites: and they that were numbered of them were forty and three thousand and seven hundred and thirty.

> Verse 12 The sons of Simeon after their families…14 These are the families of the Simeonites, twenty and two thousand and two hundred.

So about half of the strength of Reuben. You say, "Oh, that doesn't prove nothing." I'll grant you that doesn't prove anything, but look at the next son.

198

Verse 15 The children of Gad after their families...18
These are the families of the children of Gad according to
those that were numbered of them, forty thousand and five
hundred.

Tribe 1 that's mentioned in the 40s. Tribe 2 which is Simeon in the
20s. Tribe 3 which is Gad is back in the 40s. So clearly there is a
distinction in the size. A person could say that that is a reward or a
curse, a blessing or a cursing from the Lord.

Verse 22 These are the families of Judah according to those
that were numbered of them, threescore and sixteen
thousand and five hundred.

So you have in the 40s, in the 20s, in the 40s, in the 70s. So already
you can see that God is making one of the tribes more prosperous
than the others. Let's see if I can just demonstrate this here. You
have Judah, and by the way, later on they almost by themselves
have as many fighting men as the northern 10 or 11 tribes
altogether. By the time you get into the time of the kings, it is
striking how huge it is compared to the other tribes put together.
So you have Judah here and you have this sort of this average and
then you have Simeon. So that is how it's developing as we get
later into the Old Testament.

Deuteronomy 33:1 And [Moses] said, The LORD came from
Sinai, and rose up from Seir unto them; he shined forth from
mount Paran, and he came with ten thousands of saints: from his
right hand went a fiery law for them...4 Moses commanded us a
law, even the inheritance of the congregation of Jacob. And he was
king in Jeshurun, when the heads of the people and the tribes of
Israel were gathered together...6 Let Reuben live, and not die; and
let not his men be few. And this is the blessing of Judah: and he
said, Hear, LORD, the voice of Judah, and bring him unto his
people...8 And of Levi he said, Let thy Thummim and thy Urim be

199

with thy holy one..." So we have sons 1, 3 and 4 mentioned but there is no Simeon. Then verse 12, we skip around and we get son 12, and verse 13, son 11, and by the way, by the end of the chapter, Simeon is not mentioned at all and he's the only son of the 12 not mentioned as having a blessing and he's not even worth a curse.

So I don't know exactly what's taking place but it seems like whatever attitude God is reflecting through the writer of Moses on Simeon, it is what Joseph had in his opinion in Genesis 42. They diminish in Numbers 26 and they're nothing in Deuteronomy 33. I don't think I know enough to boldly say that they are non-existent by the time Jesus comes, but I think it's safe to say that they are becoming pretty insignificant by the time of Christ.[150]

I think it's significant that Reuben tries to clear his name somewhat. In the very next verse Joseph makes Simeon stick behind. I think that is a great summary. Simeon was the second born.

42:21-22

And they said one to another, We are verily guilty concerning our brother, in that we saw the anguish of his soul, when he besought us, and we would not hear; therefore is this distress come upon us. So we're getting details that weren't given to us in Genesis 37. Can you hear Joseph begging for his life and then begging to not be sold and to be sent away from home? This is really something.

22 And Reuben answered them, saying, "Spake I not unto you, saying, Do not sin against the child; and ye would not hear?" Now they don't argue with him so I have to believe it but this is something that is not found in chapter 37 either. He does speak there but not to this extent. "I told you don't sin against him and

---

[150]In Revelation 7 he makes the list again but is quite down the list.

you would not hear therefore, behold, also his blood is required." If this is true, though, it was always **Reuben**'s plan not to do anything bad to Joseph.

Now why should **Reuben**'s words have meant more?

He's the oldest. His leadership was wretched apparently to where he could not steer his brothers. He's talking to a bunch of guys in their 20s about a 17 year old brother. He should have been able to have a little more pull but what is the thing we find out about Reuben? What does Reuben do that tells us about his character? He sleeps with one of his father's wives which is some of his half-brothers' mother.

42:23-24

But they did not know that Joseph understood them, for he spoke to them through an interpreter. This reminds us of Genesis 37:12 and following where Reuben has nothing to do with the plan to harm Joseph (37:21). Then, we see here that for the first time, Joseph knows the oldest son of Jacob had nothing to do with his being sold. Verse 29 of that chapter later says he was away when the little brother was sold. He knows it was all Simeon. This is probably why Simeon is the one he keeps behind in the verses to follow. **24 And he turned himself away from them and wept. Then he returned to them again, and talked with them. And he took Simeon from them and bound him before their eyes. Simeon,** we find out from Genesis 29, is the 2nd oldest son of Jacob and was probably in charge in the absence of Reuben. Maybe Joseph is being vindictive here? "**Simeon**, I'm here because of you. You can now stay behind in Egypt for a few more days." **Simeon** may have even been the guy who wanted to kill Joseph in the first place.

Consider Numbers 26:1, and following, some 38 years after the Exodus, finds a census taking place. 26:7 discuss the Reubenites being over 43,000. **Simeon**ites, in 26:14, find about half of that. The next son listed, Gad, finds among them over 40,000. Clearly there is a distinction in the size. This could very well be a sign of cursing as much as the children of Judah being over 70,000 is a sign of their blessing. By the time you get into the times of the Kings, Judah has almost as much as the northern ten tribes together.

Then, there is Deuteronomy 33. Moses is about to die. In verse 4, the blessings begin on the tribes. **Simeon** is not mentioned at all! How did this happen? Whatever happened, it seems related to Joseph's view of **Simeon.** They diminish by Numbers 26 and disappear by Deuteronomy 33—at least in the way of blessing. On the other hand, Revelation 7 seems to have them making a comeback with their equal strength with the other tribes.

42:25-28

Then Joseph gave a command to fill their sacks with grain, to restore every man's money to his sack, and to give them provisions for the journey. Great manipulation here: **Joseph** communicates somehow with a servant to restore everybody's money without their knowledge.

27 But as one *of them* opened his sack to give his donkey feed at the encampment, They pull off at the gas station to get some drinks and such, and to their horror, they now appear to be thieves.

28 My money is restored; and, lo, it is even in my sack: and their heart failed them, and they were afraid, saying one to another, What is this that God hath done unto us? Now I just wanted to point something out here real quick, it is about 190 mile journey they had to take before they realized, "Oh my goodness!" One of them gets off at the way stop to water the beast and, "Good heavens, my money is in my bag!" And right now it looks like there's just one brother that fits that description.

I don't want to give them too much credit as being respecters of God, they've given me precious little indication that they feared Jehovah, but maybe they have enough sense here to realize that God is behind everything. Joseph, on the other hand, gives God the blame for putting Him in Egypt (chapters 45 & 50).

42:32

We be twelve brethren, sons of our father; one is not, and the youngest is this day with our father in the land of Canaan. "So one is dead and one is back home with dad."

42:34

And bring your youngest brother to me; so I shall know that you are not spies, but that you are honest men. I will grant your brother to you, and you may trade in the land.'" Once again, we see monetary interests as the motivation behind mostly everything.

42:35

And it came to pass as they emptied their sacks, that, behold, it wasn't just one dude that had his money back, **every man's bundle of money was in his sack: and when both they and their father saw the bundles of money, they were afraid.** Now why would they be afraid? It looks like they stole it. I don't know what they're thinking right now. They're afraid, I know that because as far as they know they gave the **money** to the steward and now they have their **money.** But it's interesting to note that they don't think that God was behind their selling Joseph into Egypt but we find out that God was, in fact, behind it. So the author, who is up here, Moses, is looking down on the whole story by the Holy Spirit and he says that Joseph knew that God sent him into slavery (45:5). Joseph was willing to say, "Hey, you brothers did this to me but God was doing it." So there's a lot of respecters of God's control behind the scenes and his brothers are some of them, but only as when they were in trouble.

42:36

And Jacob their father said to them, "You have bereaved me: Joseph is no *more,* and now basically, he's basically saying Simeon is as good as dead. Why is Simeon basically as good as dead? I guess **Simeon** is going to rot in an Egyptian cell because Benjamin isn't coming to this mess!

Simeon is no *more,* If they returned with Joseph's money, he would be seen as a thief anyway, so he'll probably die in prison. **and you want to take Benjamin.** Is at least 20 years old since he was born around the time of Joseph's 18th year (37:2) and Joseph is now no less than 39 (7 years of plenty have passed and probably two more of famine of gone by.).

42:37-38

Then Reuben who isn't all that honorable, having gone to bed with Bilhah (35:22), **spoke to his father, saying, "Kill my two sons if I do not bring him back to you;** Imagine a frantic family of Simeon. If **Reuben** has children so do the other brothers. Well, we know **Reuben** has children. It's probably safe to assume that Simeon, who is just probably a year, maybe two years younger than him also has children. You know, it's hard for us to think through this but this is not a church youth group missions trip down to Egypt where everyone piles out of the van taking pictures, smoking and joking with sunglasses on. These are 30 year old men and they have wives and children (at least **Reuben** did) so it seems that Simeon is being arrested and his family is frantic back home.

put him in my hands, and I will bring him back to you."

204

38 But he said, "My son shall not go down with you, for his brother is dead, and he is left alone. If any calamity should befall him along the way in which you go, then you would bring down my gray hair with sorrow to the grave." He is, by now, about 128 or 129 years old. Jacob is paying dearly for the shenanigans he played on his dad. Dishonesty breeds dishonesty—only more of it (as is declared in Galatians 6:7-8).

to the grave." This, being the counterpart to the Greek *hades* (compare Psalm 16 & Acts 2), is the realm of the dead, not the physical **grave.** If a man who is over 120 years old can say this, it speaks to the longevity of the lives back then. Dying in the near future would have been considered "before my time."

Chapter 43

43:1

And the famine was sore in the land. So they are still in Canaan and it's one of those things, you're like "maybe if we put this off another week we won't have to make a decision." I don't know if you're like that, I am. Let's sleep on it one more time. And the **famine was** still there. They have been "sleeping on it one more night" for months.

43:6

And Israel His name changed in chapter 32. **said, "Why did you deal so wrongfully with me as to tell the man whether you had still another brother?"** Can you please tell me how this happened again? They already did that because it said earlier in the previous chapter, verse 29, they told their father all that befell them. So they've already told the story and Jacob, also known as **Israel,** is making a fundamental problem that most people do today, "If I just had better understanding, I'm sure the problem would go away. If I just understood and knew how, if I understood why, if I understood everything behind it, I'm sure it would feel better." No, it won't feel better just because you know why or how something happened. Not always. I hope you see that. "I don't know why my husband did that. If I just knew." It won't make it any better.

43:7

But they said, "The man asked us pointedly about ourselves and our family, saying, 'Is your father still alive? Have you another brother?' Probably to see if they were treating his kid brother the way he was treated. **And we told him according to these words. Could we possibly have known that he would say, 'Bring your brother down'?"** "I thought we were sort of small talking. How was I to know the guy was going to say "go get your brother?"

And Judah said unto Israel his father," "I mean, we were small-talking, dad." **And Judah said unto Israel his father, Send the lad with me.** Now okay, how old is Benjamin at least? Well, he's at least 20 because he's been gone 20, he was born before Joseph was sold into slavery so Jacob is old enough to where a 20-something year old is a lad.

Then Judah said to Israel his father, "Send the lad with me, Consider Genesis 22:5. We are seeing a 20-some-year old Benjamin being called a "lad." Now consider that Abraham uses the same word for Isaac and you realize that Isaac could have been an older teenager when he was willing to die in an act of sacrifice to God performed by his father. After all, we're not told how many years have passed between Genesis 21 and 22. This speaks so highly of Isaac which speaks even higher of Christ (Whom he portrays) as a 33 year old man who died for His Father.

9 I myself will be surety for him; from my hand you shall require him. If I do not bring him back to you and set him before you, then let me bear the blame forever. This is incredibly Christological. Judah shines for the first time here. He is to be surety for the life of another. Maybe, in chapter 37, Judah was trying to keep his brother Joseph alive (although he did not attempt to sway his brothers' overall intention of ridding themselves of Joseph), but here we have explicit altruism, it seems. "I'll die if I don't make this happen."

43:11-14

And their father Israel said unto them, If it must be so now, do this; take of the best fruits in the land in your vessels. Now remember, it's not a total famine, there's still fruit but if you eat fruit.... Alright, so there is a certain limit to how much fruit and nuts you want to ingest, okay? Business will pick up for you if you overdo that, okay?

12 And take double money in your hand; and the money that was brought again in the mouth of your sacks, carry it again in your hand; peradventure it was an oversight. "Maybe it was just an oversight."

14 And may God Almighty give you mercy This is the first time Jacob has given this name *(El Shaddai)* to God. He appears to be invoking the Almighty quality of God while acknowledging his own lack of ability and control (in the next phrase). **before the man, that he may release your other brother and Benjamin. If I am bereaved, I am bereaved!"** This is neither fatalistic or hurried manipulation of the situation. This appears to be a desperate faith.

14 And God Almighty give you mercy before the man, that he may send away your other brother, and Benjamin. If I be bereaved of my children, I am bereaved. Two things here. 1. Why do you suppose he's using the *term El Shaddai*, or **God Almighty**? This is the first time Jacob has ever spoken that name for God, at least in our biblical record. Why is he now deciding to use that name to speak of what God may do, what we hope he does?

43:23

But he said, "Peace *be* with you, do not be afraid. Your God and the God of your father has given you treasure in your sacks; I had your money." So Joseph's steward lied at Joseph's direction, and we should consider this as perhaps, Joseph's one recorded sin.

43:26

And when Joseph came home, so this is the second time the brothers have come to Egypt. What are the differences in the construct of the crowd that is traveling from Canaan to Egypt?

Benjamin is with them.

And who is not with them?

Simeon is not.

Where is Simeon? Jail. Right.

43:27

Then he asked them about *their* well-being, and said, "*Is* your father well, the old man of whom you spoke? *Is* he still alive?" Jacob, we will find, comes to Egypt at 130 years of age so here is a man who is nearly 130 years old, having not seen him for 20 years.

43:29

Then he lifted his eyes and saw his brother Benjamin, his mother's son, and said, "*Is* this your younger brother of whom you spoke to me?" And he said, "God Remember that this is the English translation of the Hebrew translation of Joseph's Egyptian language. **be gracious to you, my son."** Joseph being 6 or 7 years old when they leave uncle Laban's and nearly 10 years passing before Benjamin's birth, this term **son** is more about position than age difference.

43:32

And they set on for him by himself, and for them by themselves, and for the Egyptians, which did eat with him, by themselves: because the Egyptians might not eat bread with the Hebrews; for that is an abomination unto the Egyptians." I think this is really humorous if you try to get there in your imagination. "Let's eat together...at separate tables."

43:33

And they sat before him, the firstborn according to his birthright, and the youngest according to his youth: and the men marvelled one at another. Can you see it? They're sitting and eating very well and they're looking at each other in amazement. What do you think? What kind of amazement are we talking about here? "Do you believe this?"

43:34

And [Joseph] took and sent messes unto them from before him. I'm kind of getting the idea Joseph has his presidential spread because he's number 2 in the land, effectively number 2 in the world when it comes to resource management, and it seems like they're taking the food from his table and taking it to the brothers and Benjamin got five times as much as they did **and they drank and were merry with him.** Now they're sitting in order of their birth and down at the end is Did they do that on their own? Did he set it that way? It could be that they sat that way naturally. Maybe that was the custom. You know, if you're the oldest, you sit up here and you sit in order of your birth. Who knows? Remember, Benjamin is probably 20 years junior to some of these other brothers. He might be 22 years old at this time, 23 years old, but he's still the lad, and he has five times as much stuff in front of him.

Rachel is Jacob's right hand and he calls Benjamin "son of my right hand." Well, where is Jesus today, Son of God? He is at the right hand of God. So we already know based on that previous story, and oh, by the way, Benjamin becomes alive right outside what town where the Son of the right hand of God comes alive? You know I'm talking about birth, not conception. I've got my stuff

210

right here. I know life began in Nazareth for Jesus but where was he born?

Yeah, Bethlehem

and where did Rachel die?

Ramah, right north of Bethlehem while she's giving birth to Benjamin.

Would the brothers be having this meal with Joseph if Benjamin was not in the picture? The brothers get to eat with the king, the brothers get to eat with the king because the man in charge favors the least esteemed brother and wants Benjamin in his presence. He also wants the brothers in his presence, or we could just make a beeline for the bottom line, there would be no meal for the others if Benjamin wasn't involved. So that is a huge picture of Jesus.

Being a part of the kingdom is an impossibility if it were not for the least esteemed among our brethren, Jesus, and because he is the star of the show during the coming big dance, so to speak, we get to be there and we get to share in the fact that the Father wants to honor the Son, and because he wants to honor the Son and we are recipients with the Son, we get to be honored with him and that is what is happening here.

Joseph is the second person called a Hebrew in the book of Genesis (39:14; 40:15). 14:13 finds Abram being called a "Hebrew."

"Hebrew" may have developed into the meaning of a wanderer but let's see how it started:

> Genesis 10:21 Unto Shem also, the father of all the children of Eber, the brother of Japheth the elder, even to him were children born.

211

Now he had more sons in Eber because look at verse 22

> *The children of Shem; Elam, and Asshur, and Arphaxad,*
> *and Lud, and Aram....24And Arphaxad begat Salah; and*
> *Salah begat Eber...*

Basically, if you were a son of this line of Shem, you were a
Hebrew, Eber. If you were a son of Shem, that means you're
Semitic, it used to be Shemitic but then they dropped the "h." It's
Semitic. So when we say that, "Oh, that tribe is Semitic," we're
saying they're from this third of Noah's lineage. Semitic, but
genetically the Hebrews were the line of Eber from Shem. So now
you know where the term Hebrew came from.

Chapter 44

44:2-5

And put my cup, the silver cup, which by the way in the preceding chapter, the word "money" in my translation anyways is the same word **silver**. So this is little bags of silver in their bags.

2 And put my cup, the silver cup, in the sack's mouth of the youngest, He does it again, Joseph does, after he gives his little brother a heaping portion in comparison with his other brothers.

4 And when they were gone out of the city, and not yet far off, Joseph said unto his steward, Up, follow after the men; and when thou dost overtake them, say unto them, Wherefore have ye rewarded evil for good? They got Simeon back and got grain twice and ate meals together and Joseph's people are now using that against them. **5 Is not this it in which my lord drinketh, and whereby indeed he divineth?** It is a "special cup" that is thought to have revealed the future to him. **ye have done evil in so doing.** One looks into this **divin**ing cup and puts fluid in it and you would add things to it and then the fluid would behave a little bit and you'd be able to tell the future by how the fluid or the liquid behaved in this cup.

44:9

With whomsoever of thy servants it be found, both let him die, and we also will be my lord's bondmen. Now, how dumb. Who in the world would say that? You've got your 10 brothers with you and you're saying things like, "Well, wherever you find it, let them die and the rest of us will serve you." He must have been a very confident man for whatever reason.

44:12-15

And he searched, and began at the eldest, for dramatic effect, "I'm gonna start way up here," **and the cup was found in Benjamin's sack. 13 Then they rent their clothes,** here, they had just had gotten Simeon restored to them and now, dad's favorite has been implicated. **15 And Joseph said unto them, "What deed is this that ye have done? Did you not know, that such a man as I can certainly divine?"** I can tell the future. Do you not know that I knew that you took it? I even have a divining cup, do you not know that I knew that you took my divining cup?" Again, we need to talk about whether this is dishonesty. Is this like psychological operations within national defense and therefore, justifiable (I say this as a matter of representation of those who would say so)?

44:16

Then Judah said, "What shall we say to my lord? What shall we speak? Or how shall we clear ourselves? God has found out the iniquity of your servants; here we are, my lord's slaves, both we and *he* also with whom the cup was found." Here, then, is the 2nd time Joseph had something planted in the baggage of others.

44:17

And he said, God forbid that I should do so: but the man in whose hand the cup is found, he shall be my servant; and as for you, get you up in peace unto your father. "Hey, don't worry about it. I'll just keep the one of whom we found the cup." Maybe Joseph plans to ultimately have Benjamin with him in Egypt? Is he trying to protect his little brother from these awful men?

Do we have any proof that Joseph himself actually practiced this? Not really. Do we have any indication that he probably didn't? What do we know he was able to do that was kind of supernatural? Interpret dreams. We find no evidence that he needed a divining cup to do that, right?

214

Deuteronomy 18:10 There shall not be found among you any one that maketh his son or his daughter to pass through the fire, or that useth divination, or an observer of times, or an enchanter, or a witch, Or a charmer, or a consulter with familiar spirits or a wizard, or a necromancer for all that do these things are an abomination unto the LORD: and because of these abominations the LORD thy God doth drive them out from before thee.

So what is clear is that Moses wrote the account of Joseph and Moses wrote the account of Deuteronomy within 40 years of each other, and in any case, you see what God thinks about divination.

44:18

Then Judah came near to him and said: "O my lord, please let your servant speak a word in my lord's hearing, and do not let your anger burn against your servant; for you *are* even like Pharaoh. This is how important Joseph is on the world stage.

44:20-22

And we said to my lord, 'We have a father, an old man, and a child of *his* old age, *who is* young; his brother is dead, and he alone is left of his mother's children, and his father loves him.' This is the first argument of their honesty (the other being their returning of Joseph's money from their first trip to Egypt): Joseph's character wouldn't even know about Benjamin if he had not asked and these men were not telling the truth.

22 And we said to my lord, 'The lad cannot leave his father, for *if* he should leave his father, *his father* would die.' Joseph, then, is getting good proof that his father is still alive. Maybe Joseph sees the possibility of not only caring for Benjamin, but also his father?

44:29

But if you take this one also from me, and calamity befalls him, you shall bring down my gray hair with sorrow to the grave.' If we did not have all the rehearsals of things (dreams) to 3ʳᵈ parties, I wonder how long Genesis would be? This happens with Acts 10 and 11.

44:33

Now therefore, please ˣlet your servant remain instead of the lad as a slave to my lord, and let the lad go up with his brothers. It seems that this is the place where Judah takes prominence in the story. Here he is willing to be a substitute to suffer for the crimes (although merely perceived) of another.

ˣEx. 32:32

Chapter 45

If we didn't have the opening verses of chapter 37 we would think Joseph is the main character of the story and that this portion of Scripture was the climax, but since we know that this portion of the book is about "the generations of Jacob" (37:2), we know to keep reading.

45:1-2

Then Joseph could not restrain himself before all those who stood by him, and he cried out, These last two or three chapters were the process of guiding his brothers into repentance while he himself had to have a real sense of Providence...which is evident in verse 8.

2 And he wept aloud, and the Egyptians and the house of Pharaoh heard *it*. If you were assigned to keep Joseph safe, what would you think once you were put out and **heard weep**ing?

45:3-8

Then Joseph said to his brothers, "I *am* Joseph; does my father still live?" Jacob would believe a lie until his dying day if it were not for **Joseph's** persistence with **his brothers**

4 And Joseph said to his brothers, "Please come near to me." So they came near. Then he said: "I *am* Joseph your brother, Joseph was probably fixed up like a world-empire despot (and of course it had been 22 years since his **brother**s had gotten rid of him).

6 For these two years the famine This means we are 9 years past his first time before Pharaoh. This makes Joseph 39 and his father around 130 years old.

7 And God sent me before you We will never help anybody as counselor if we don't quickly point to **God**'s involvement in the big picture.

to preserve a [1]posterity for you in the earth Joseph said they would not be looking at each other for him to save them if they had not sinned. What room is there for regret? There is no salvation for Joseph's brothers if they don't sin in the first place. In the salvation meta-narrative of Scripture, nobody who is perfect has a Savior. Joseph can feed the whole world because of the sins of his brother. This is so Christ-like. See Zechariah 12:10 & 13:6 as a place to consider this. John 20:21 is beautiful thing, given the disciples' failure to stick it out with Jesus.

8 So now *it was* not you *who* sent me here, but God We would rather say "Joseph was a poor theologian." However, he walked with **God** for some time and knew the character of Christ. **God sent**—through hatred, envy, indiscretion, bitterness, slavery, Ishmaelites (and therefore adultery), favoritism, or any kind of wickedness—this man to Egypt.

and He has made me a father to Pharaoh, he married the daughter of a priest so maybe that is why he is called **a father**? He was known, after all, as a diviner.

45:22-24

He gave to all of them, to each man, changes of garments; but to Benjamin he gave three hundred *pieces* of silver and five changes of garments. And this is after he gave his little brother five times the food in 43:34. **23 And he sent to his father these *things:* ten donkeys** there were **ten** camels in Genesis 24 while Laban changed Jacob's wages **ten** times (Genesis 31

---

[1]remnant

24 So he sent his brothers away, and they departed; and he said to them, "See that you do not become troubled this word is only used once and seems like there is a chiding for what quarreling may take place.

45:26-27

And they told him, saying, "Joseph *is* still alive, and he *is* governor over all the land of Egypt." All of the sudden, this poor old man feels like this is one more tale being told by his sons. It's far-fetched. Not only that, but what a story! The man who strong-armed them is the guy who was their brother? **And Jacob's heart stood still, because he did not believe them.** His son was mangled by beasts (he thinks) and **27 But when they told him all the words which Joseph had said to them, and when he saw the carts which Joseph had sent to carry him** Jacob actually has permission to go to Egypt in the midst of a famine, unlike his father (Genesis 26:1) and his grandfather (Genesis 12:10). This is about timing then.

28 Then Israel said, "*It is* enough. Joseph my son *is* still alive. I will go and see him before I die." 47:27 tells us that he lives another 17 years. This seems like another similarity between **Joseph** and Jesus (see the story of Simeon in Luke 2).

Chapter 46

46:1-2

So Israel took his journey with all that he had, and came to Beersheba, named such in Genesis 26. The last time he was there was in 28:10. He was not married and therefore did not have children. This was probably 53 years ago. Since we cannot assume he had never returned for anything, we must assume the writer is attempting to communicate with the reader. In both cases, though, Jacob is leaving Canaan.

46:3-7

So He said, "I *am* God, the God of your father; do not fear to go down to Egypt, One of the reasons he might fear is because of his father's and grandfather's own stories of trips to **Egypt** (Genesis 12 and Genesis 26). Another great reason is that Jacob might be wondering how to regain possession for his land in this "Promised Land."

4 I will go down with you to Egypt Just as God went with Joseph (39:2). Either God left **Egypt** (and Joseph) or He is omnipresent. **and I will also surely bring you up *again*** He comes up in a coffin or "box of bones," though. **and Joseph will put his hand on your eyes."** Another way of saying that **Joseph** would be there when he (Jacob) died.

7 His sons and his sons' sons, his daughters and his sons' daughters, and all his descendants he brought with him to Egypt. So, **his daughters**-in-law are not included.

46:8-15[151]

---

[151]See under 38:25-26.

I wanted to suggest something, perhaps, a little more easy to swallow on the difference between the 66 and the 70 of Genesis 46:26-27. I suggested that it were Ephraim, Manassah, Er, and Onan that made up the four, but I needed to be honest with myself following the lesson and see that Exodus 1 says "70" and it removes all doubt that these "70" came into Egypt. So, since, Genesis 47:27 tells us #'s 67 and 68 are Ephraim and Manassah, but you may also notice that Jacob could be added to the "66" to make "69." Also, if you see Genesis 46:15, you will notice Dinah is not included in the "66" can also be included in the "70." Anyway, I think the difference between the 66 and the 70 may be better said as "Ephraim, Manassah, Jacob, and Dinah."

9 The sons of Reuben *were* **Hanoch,** same as Enoch—one of four in the Bible.

10 The sons of Simeon You can see the sons are mentioned in order of their birth, then. *were* **Jemuel, Jamin, Ohad, Jachin, Zohar** also the name of the person who sold land to his great great grandfather (Genesis 23).

12 The sons of Judah *were* **Er, Onan, Shelah, Perez, and Zerah (but Er and Onan died in the land of Canaan). The sons of Perez were Hezron** the second one in this caravan (46:10).

13 The sons of Issachar *were* **Tola, Puvah, Job** not the same word as the famous one.

15 These *were* **the sons of Leah, whom she bore to Jacob in Padan Aram, with his daughter Dinah. All the persons, his sons and his daughters,** *were* **thirty-three.** Listed among them is two women: **Leah** and **Dinah.** Below you will notice that verses 16-18 lists only one additional woman: **Zilpah.** Perhaps it was more than these males plus four women that went to Egypt—even though it would be actually many more, probably, than 70.

221

46:18-22

These *were* the sons of Zilpah, whom Laban gave to Leah his daughter since **Zilpah** is part of the relationship with **Leah.** She is listed before Rachel in 46:19. **and these she bore to Jacob: sixteen persons.** A total of 50 with Jacob (and those in verse 15). **22 These *were* the sons of Rachel, who were born to Jacob: fourteen persons in all.** With the math under verse 18, we now have 64 total people.

46:25-28

These *were* the sons of Bilhah, whom Laban gave to Rachel his daughter, and she bore these to Jacob: seven persons in all.** We now have 71 (with the math under verse 22). **26 All the persons who went with** or "belonged to" **Jacob to Egypt**

27 And the sons of Joseph who were born to him in Egypt *were* two persons. All the persons of the house of Jacob who went to Egypt grammatically this phrase could be describing **Jacob** or **the 70.** In other words the **70** could be either those of **the house of Jacob** or **those who went to Egypt.** Acts 7:14 says there were 75 which may include wives not included in this passage.

were seventy. Counting the wives and Jacob we get to **70.** So counting **70** in this verse we get down to "66" could be gotten down to 66 two ways: 1. Don't count the wives or Jacob (verse 26); or 2. Subtract, verse verse 26, Er and Onan. They did not get **to Egypt** and get us down to 68. It seems as though Joseph's sons (verse 20), since they did not migrate **to Egypt,** get us down to 66.

28 Then he sent Judah before him to Joseph, to point out before him *the way* to Goshen. And they came to the land of Goshen. Nearly as close to the Mediterranean Sea on the Nile River as one can get. 47:4 seems to show that this became a permanent arrangement by the request of Jacob.

222

that you shall say, 'Your servants' occupation has been with livestock He is told to tell the head man that they are the very kind of people he wants nowhere near himself. Consequently, they are given some of the most fertile land in the whole country (47:11).

Chapter 47

47:1-3

**3 Then Pharaoh said to his brothers, "What *is* your
occupation?" And they said to Pharaoh, "Your servants *are*
shepherds,** we heard in an earlier chapter that Egyptians wouldn't
even eat with **shepherds** so this may have been a sneaky way to
get them as far away from **Pharaoh** as possible. Verse 11 tells us
where this happens and it plays into Exodus 1:12 where they are
still building—making 47:11 a proleptic label for a town yet to be
built.

47:9-12[152]

**And Jacob said to Pharaoh, "The days of the years of my
pilgrimage *are* one hundred and thirty years; few** 130 years are
few. Compared to his father (who lived 180 years) and his
grandfather (175 years) and his great grandfather (205),[153] his
feelings of 45:28 make him expect his death sooner rather than
later. **and evil** After being chased by Esau (Genesis 28)[154] and
Laban (Genesis 31) while caring for a large family with its internal
strife, these days may have seem quite **evil.** This doesn't even
count the calamity of his favorite son (Genesis 37); don't forget the
bloodbath his two oldest sons caused, causing continual moving
(Genesis 34). Then, his favorite wife, whom he loved, died in
transit during birth (Genesis 35).

**10 So Jacob blessed Pharaoh, and went out from before
Pharaoh.** It appears that here the king of Egypt acknowledges the
source of this **blessing,** which is the God of Joseph and his father,
Jacob. This is not a surprise after Joseph has lived so distinctly
before him as his second in command.

---

[152]See under 47:1-3.
[153]Genesis 11:32.
[154]And we're not quite sure if any worthwhile reunion took place, other
than Genesis 32.

11 And Joseph situated his father and his brothers, and gave them a possession in the land of Egypt, in the best of the land, in the land of Rameses, Jacob and his other sons, then, have travlled roughly 250 miles from their home to this.

12 Then Joseph provided his father, his brothers, and all his father's household with bread, according to the number in *their* families. The previous chapter showed us that they had different amounts of children and Benjamin had the most (46:21).

47:29

When the time drew near that Israel must die, he called his son Joseph and said to him, "Now if I have found favor in your sight, please put your hand under my thigh This also gets mentioned in 24:3 and refers to a touching of the private area to "meet in promise" on the "seed." This was a promise of posterity related to the source of the promise, humanly speaking: the loins. Another way to say it is that the "mark of the covenant" is the point of promise. Or…circumcision, the covenantal mark between God and Abraham is on the…here we go…penis and thus this act of covenant agreement between Jacob and Joseph was actually a memorial of the first circumcision found in Genesis 17.

Chapter 48

48:1-7

2 And Jacob was told, "Look, your son Joseph is coming to you"; and Israel strengthened himself and sat up on the bed. Remember from the last chapter that he is 147 years old.

4 and said to me, 'Behold, I will make you fruitful and multiply you, this happened on his way out of Haran, some 48 years previous. **and I will make of you a multitude of people, and give this land to your descendants after you *as* an everlasting** an apparent extension of reality to the horizon of time. We would not say that there is no end to the **possession.'** Why? The easiest answer is that the old heavens will be passed away (Revelation 20:11-12; 21:1). **5 And now your two sons, Ephraim and Manasseh, who were born to you in the land of Egypt before I came to you in Egypt, *are* mine; as Reuben and Simeon** or like his first two sons—which affects inheritance. They furthermore count for their own tribes. They were both missing and complicit during the sale of Joseph. Then, **Reuben** slept with one of his stepmothers (49:4; 1 Chronicles 5:1).

7 But as for me, when I came from Padan, Rachel died beside me in the land of Canaan on the way, when *there was* but a little distance to go to Ephrath; and I buried her there on the way to Ephrath (that is, probably added by Moses **Bethlehem)."** Micah 5:2 uses both terms in its prophecy of the birth of Jesus.

48:8

Then Israel saw Joseph's sons, and said, "Who *are* these?" How could he have blessed them and not know **who** they are? 48:10 gives us the answer and this reminds us of 27:1.

48:13-14

And Joseph took them both, Ephraim with his right hand as he is facing Jacob, **Joseph** is taking his 2nd born **toward Israel's left hand, and Manasseh with his left hand toward Israel's right hand,** These are not toddlers so **Joseph** must have been a stout fellow. **and brought** *them* **near him.** Joseph is seeking to guide his firstborn to the **right hand** of his father, the position of highest blessing. **14 Then Israel stretched out his right hand and laid** *it* **on Ephraim's head,** to relive what he himself experienced as the 2nd born of Isaac. Romans 5:20 is a Bible-wide revelation of what soteriology was being taught here. **who** *was* **the younger, and his left hand on Manasseh's head, guiding his hands knowingly, for Manasseh** *was* **the firstborn.** Hebrews 11:21 remove all doubt that Jacob knew what he was doing here.

48:19

But his father refused and said, "I know, my son, I know. He also shall become a people, and he also shall be great; but truly his younger brother shall be greater than he, and his descendants shall become a multitude of nations." Jacob is then intending on replaying what happened to him as the 2nd born being blessed over his older brother Esau (in Genesis 25).

Chapter 49

49:8-10

"Shiloh" of Genesis 49:8-10 is used but once and is distinct in from the location only slightly in the Hebrew but to the point where "Shiloh" which means "tranquility" can be simply be "until peace comes."

49:31-33

There they buried Abraham recorded in chapter 25. **and Sarah his wife,** This is recorded in chapter 23. **there they buried Isaac and Rebekah his wife,** Their burials' location is not heretofore mentioned. In fact **Rebekah'**s death is not heretofore mentioned.

33 And when Jacob had finished commanding his sons, he drew his feet up into the bed and breathed his last, and was gathered to his people. This either means that he was buried in the same cave mentioned in verse 30,[155] or it is a reference to Heaven (which would introduce other questions),[156] or is it a reference to a "family receiving,"[157] or could it be a general reference to "the world of the dead?"

---

[155]Genesis 25:7, though, shows us it is not merely a reference to the family cemetery back at the cave—since the same terminology is used and only Sarah is buried there.

[156]The interesting thing is that Moses probably was actually convincing people of life after death with this simple kind of writing exemplified here (Luke 16:27-31); my friend Walter Holt brought this up in Sunday School at Berean Baptist Church (October 2015).

[157]Moreover, this can't be a reference to a family receiving, as in today's sense of a reception or a "wake," but **his sons** were already present.

Chapter 50

50:2

And Joseph commanded his servants the physicians to embalm his father. So the physicians embalmed Israel. We don't really know what this involved exactly, but what is clear to the reader is that this isn't the same as what we do today. Nevertheless, it was thorough and will most certainly be dealt with on resurrection morning.

50:15-17

When Joseph's brothers saw that their father was dead, they said, "Perhaps Joseph will hate us, and may actually repay us for all the evil which we did to him." They fear that **Joseph** may have only respected their lives thus far because dad was no longer alive to find out what he might do to them. **16 So they sent** *messengers* **to Joseph, saying, "Before your father died he commanded,** They are probably making this up. **saying, 17 'Thus you shall say to Joseph: "I beg you, please forgive the trespass of your brothers and their sin; for they did evil to you." ' Now, please, forgive the trespass of the servants of the God of your father."** Perhaps the brothers are appealing to the higher authority in **Joseph**'s life—reminding him of the God that ran his dad's life. **And Joseph wept when they spoke to him.** He has had 39 years to forgive them—17 of which they lived in the same region—and they still doubt his heart. 47:11shows us they received the "best of the land." They superimpose their character onto their brother. This is nothing but proof that to accuse somebody is often to confess of our own shortcomings.

50:20-26

But as for you, you meant evil against me; *but* **God meant it for good, in order to bring it about as** *it is* **this day, to save many people alive.** This very much echoes 45:5-8.

229

23 Joseph saw Ephraim's children to the third *generation*. **The children of Machir, the son of Manasseh, were also brought up on Joseph's knees.** Knowing that Abraham didn't see his 4th generation as **Joseph**, did (It was **Ephraim's third**). **24 And Joseph said to his brethren, "I am dying; but God will surely visit you, and bring you out of this land** first promised to his father (46:1)—proving that nobody naturally thought in singular generations.

25 Then Joseph took an oath probably in the same way this has happened so far ("hand under the thigh"). **from the children of Israel, saying, "God will surely visit you, and you shall carry up my bones from here."** He wants to wake up in God's promised land at the resurrection. **26 So Joseph died,** *being* **one hundred and ten years old;** 56 when his father died so 54 years of no record. **and they embalmed him** Significantly different than today. His was probably like Jacob's in that the internals were probably removed, as were the brains and substituted with spices. **and he was put in a coffin** otherwise translated "ark" as in "ark of the covenant" (versus the "ark" in Noah's story). **in Egypt.** Beautiful commentary can be found in Psalm 106:17-25, Acts 7:9-18, and Hebrews 11:21-22.

Made in the USA
Columbia, SC
11 June 2024